More Funky Things to Draw

Glitz & Glamour

Paul Könye • Kate Ashforth

More Funky Things to Draw

Glitz & Glamour

INTRODUCTION

Many people dream of becoming a movie star, rock star, or fashion model: wearing fabulous clothes, attending important events, greeting adoring fans from the stage or strutting along a catwalk. Celebrities enjoy a glamorous and glitzy lifestyle, though it comes with a few strings attached. If you become a star, you'll find that all the details of your personal life will be reported in magazines, and people will take your picture and ask for your autograph everywhere you go!

THINGS YOU WILL NEED

- A gray lead pencil (HB or 2B).
- A pencil sharpener and a dish for shavings.
- Sheets of drawing paper.
- A clean eraser.
- Patience—learning drawing skills takes time and practice.
- Confidence—a positive attitude will help to develop your drawing skills!

Drawing Guidelines

1 There is a process in learning to draw. Follow the steps carefully and in order.
2 Always use light pencil pressure when beginning the first stage of a drawing.
3 If you feel unsure about the instructions, ask an adult for help.
4 Gray lead smudges easily. Pay attention to where your hand is on the page.
5 Clean the gray lead residue off your eraser by rubbing it against a spare piece of paper.
6 Most of the directions for drawing people don't mention the joints of the limbs or the hand and feet shapes, but they're still important! Be sure to draw them in.

 Beginner Intermediate  Expert

The stars at the top of each page grade the difficulty level of each drawing from beginner to intermediate or expert. Some drawings are trickier than others because of the level of detail, but if you carefully follow the basic principles of building a drawing from shapes and lines, you will learn to conquer both simple and complex drawings.

Follow the Steps

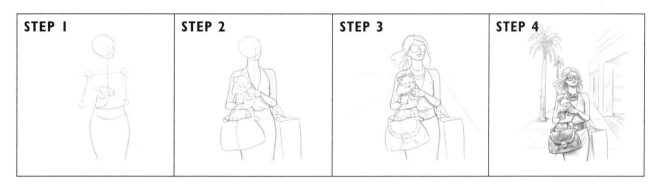

Throughout the following pages, you will find a variety of human subjects. To draw the human form, you need to construct a "skeleton" using a series of joints, lines, and shapes. The form of each subject is shaped around the skeleton using a curved outline. Study the shapes and joints that are drawn for the skeleton and the lengths of all the lines. Observe the line and curve of the spine and the positions and angles of all the body parts.

PENCIL TECHNIQUES FOR DRAWING PEOPLE

The boxes below show a variety of lines drawn for a subject.

direction of line   flowing lines   irregular shapes

When you arrive at each page of this book, observe the different types of lines drawn for each subject. Are they wavy, curved, or irregular? Also, look at the width of all lines, and their direction.

The positioning of lines for the spine, shoulders, and hips gives a human figure its balance and structure. Light to medium pencil pressure is used to create a thin or thick line and to give fabric or hair a sense of movement.

Shading and Pencil Pressure

Shading adds detail and definition to a subject. Apply different levels of shading with changes in pencil pressure—a light pencil grip creates a light gray tone, for example.

The boxes below show different levels of gray tone created by a pencil.

Light   Medium   Dark

More Funky Things to Draw—Glitz & Glamour

POP STAR ⭐

The "pop" in "pop star" and "pop music" means "popular." Pop music is designed to appeal to a wide audience, making it perfect for playing on the radio and in dance clubs. Pop songs are usually short and catchy, with lyrics that stick in your mind and a beat that will get you moving. Pop singers tour around the world performing concerts and promoting their hit songs (sometimes called "singles") and albums. The most popular pop singers can become worldwide megastars!

Before You Begin

The pop star's form is built around a skeleton. The lines showing the angles of the singer's shoulders, hips, and knees are parallel. To draw her pose correctly, it is important that you position her body parts in the right way. Observe closely the positioning of her head, arms, hands, and feet.

Step 1

Lightly draw a circle for the head. Draw the face cross at an angle and add a chin shape underneath. Draw a spine coming down at a slight angle. For the chest and hips, draw two ellipses at the same angle. Sketch the shoulders, and on your left draw a bent arm. Draw the other arm bent over the chest with the hand overlapping the chin. Sketch the bent front leg with a block shape for the shoe. Then draw the leg behind. Notice that the rear shoe is just above the front one.

Step 2

Draw a curved outline around the skeleton. Start at the neck and work your way down to her shoes. Observe that she has a band around her hips and that the leg on your left sits slightly behind the front leg.

hand overlaps chin

parallel lines

arm overlaps chest

parallel lines

parallel lines

band around hips

rear shoe slightly above

leg sits behind

fingers curl over

wavy hair around shoulders

open palm

heels inside block shapes

Step 3

Draw wavy hair around the pop star's head and shoulders. Sketch her eyes on either side of the cross. Follow with her nose and the top of her mouth. Sketch her fingers inside the hand shapes. Observe how her fingers curl over and her palms are open. Draw her bangles, and her microphone pointing outward. Define her shirt, belt, and jeans. Draw her boots, sketching the heels inside the block shapes.

DRAWING TIP

When drawing a checked floor pattern, make sure that the lines that go across the page are closer together at the back and become more open near the front of the picture.

Step 4

Study the levels of shading over the pop star's figure. Using light pencil pressure, shade the wavy texture of her hair. Define her facial features, bangles, and belt. Softly shade her skin and the folds running down her top. Shade light gray tone across her jeans and boots, leaving white areas clear. Once you draw the checked pattern for the dance floor and the lights shining behind, your pop star will be ready to sing!

INTERESTING FACT → Michael Jackson was one of the most famous musicians in the world. His 1982 album *Thriller* is the biggest-selling album of all time.

MALE MODEL ★ ★ ☆

Male models are an important part of the fashion industry, as they are needed to show male collections and to be the face of products that are designed especially for men. Just like women, men have to work hard to stay fit and healthy to work in the modeling industry, and are chosen to promote fashion designers' new collections on runways in New York, Milan, and Paris.

Before You Begin

Observe that the drawing of the male model is built around a blocky suit shape. To achieve the right pose, you must draw his shoulders and hips at the correct angles. Pay attention to the angles of the knees and the different positions of the legs and shoes.

Step 1

Lightly draw a circle for the head with a long chin shape. Draw a cross for the face. Then add angled shoulders below. Draw a chest shape that nips in at the waist, and then draw the hip area. Draw arm shapes with hands at either side of the torso. Note how one hand hides behind the hip. Sketch the straight leg with a rounded foot shape. Draw the bent leg, sketching the calf area that narrows toward the ankle. Make sure the knees are in line with each other and the pointed foot is above the baseline.

Step 2

Create the outline of the model's suit. Start at the shoulders, adding the jacket opening and the vest underneath. Work your way down to his shoes, creating folds in the suit as you go. Pay attention to the large folds around the bent leg. Don't forget the cuffs around the wrists and ankles.

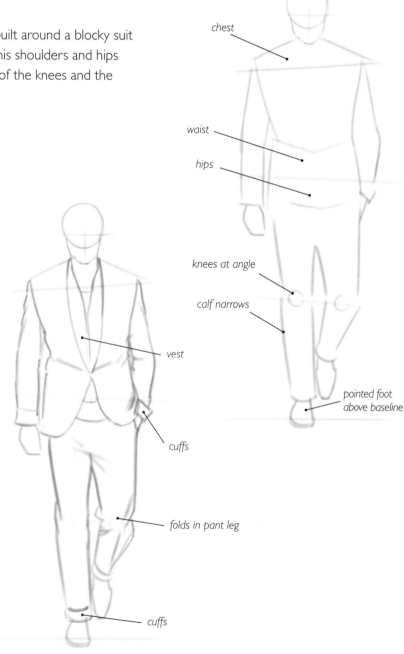

chest

waist

hips

knees at angle

calf narrows

pointed foot above baseline

vest

cuffs

folds in pant leg

cuffs

Step 3

Define and darken the outline of the model's suit, adding further folds around his waist. Draw his facial features on either side of the cross. Then draw his ears and hair. Add notched lapels, buttons and pockets to the suit. Draw fingers inside the hand shape. Sketch his shirt under the jacket, define his neck, and add detail to the shoes.

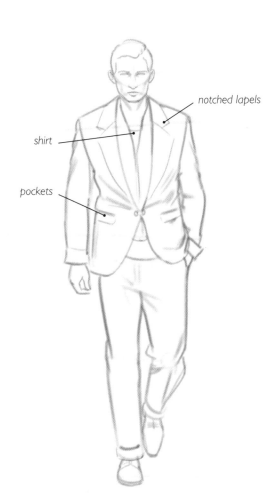

notched lapels

shirt

pockets

DRAWING TIP

When drawing facial features over a cross, always begin with the eyes. This will help you draw the nose and mouth the right distance apart.

Step 4

Using light pencil pressure, build up shading on his hair and define his facial features. Add a soft bumpy texture to his vest. Starting at the shoulders, add light highlights in the suit. Darken his shirt and shoes. Once you draw the catwalk in the background, your male model will be ready to stride!

INTERESTING FACT → Famous sportsmen like David Beckham can be paid millions of dollars to model a company's product in advertisements.

SOCIALITE ★ ★

A socialite is a wealthy or beautiful person who attends noted social events and parties. A socialite always wears designer clothing and loves being photographed by the paparazzi. Promoters of parties often pay socialites lots of money to attend their events and make them look exciting and fashionable. Many socialites use their fame and connections to launch product lines and raise money for charitable causes.

Before You Begin

The drawing of the socialite and her Chihuahua is built using a series of shapes and lines. To draw your socialite's pose correctly, you must draw her head, shoulders, and arms at the correct angles. Observe how the arms are bent and crossing over her torso. The arm on your left is slightly lower. Study all the steps before you start so you can see how the Chihuahua is drawn.

Step 1

Lightly draw a circle for the head. Draw a chin shape below and then a cross for the face, looking to your right. Sketch a slightly curved spine and then a skirt shape below. Draw an oval for the chest, with shoulders at a slight angle across the top. Draw the bent arm on your left, with the elbow pointing out slightly and the open hand sitting on the hip. Sketch the other bent arm crossing her torso.

Step 2

Starting at the neck, draw the outline of the socialite's form around the skeleton. Draw the outline of her halter-neck top and the boxy shopping bag. Sketch the dog's head and fur jacket. Draw its tail and foot underneath the arm. Then add the socialite's handbag.

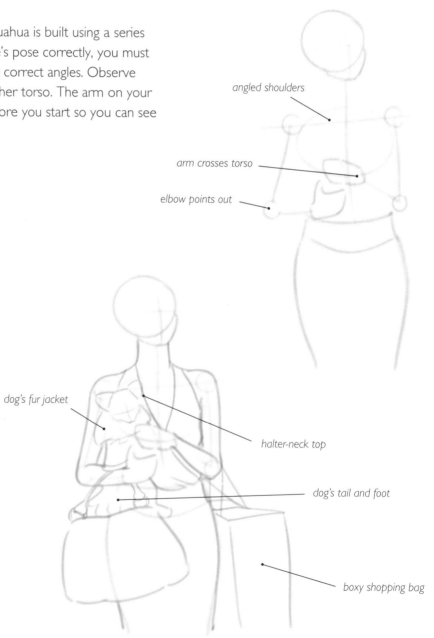

angled shoulders

arm crosses torso

elbow points out

dog's fur jacket

halter-neck top

dog's tail and foot

boxy shopping bag

squarish sunglasses

hair is moving

belt buckle

handbag flap

Step 3

Draw wispy and wavy lines of hair around her head to make it look like it's moving. Draw squarish sunglasses over her eyes and add her nose, mouth, and ear. Draw curved lines for a necklace and draw fingers inside the hand shapes. Draw her circular belt buckle and the flap and latch of the handbag. Create the fine, furry texture of the dog's hair and jacket and draw its bow and face.

DRAWING TIP

To keep your drawing clean, turn your page as you sketch to draw different elements of your picture. This way you will prevent smudging!

Step 4

Darken and define the socialite's outline and facial features. Using fine lines, add further texture to her hair. Draw oval beads around her neckline and define the dog's face and fur. Add pattern to the handbag flap and latch. Starting at her head, use light pencil pressure to add different levels of shading over her figure. Using perspective, draw the details of the shopping strip larger in the foreground and smaller in the distance. Now your socialite is ready to pose!

INTERESTING FACT → Paris Hilton, Nicole Richie, and Kim Kardashian are young socialites who have made careers out of their popularity.

More Funky Things to Draw—Glitz & Glamour

CELEBRITY COUPLE ★★★

Paparazzi is an Italian term that refers to photojournalists who specialize in taking candid photographs of celebrities. They often intrude on a celebrity's personal life, following them to parties, stores, vacations, and restaurants. Some have also been known to go through a celebrity's trash to learn their secrets. Paparazzi always have a car or motorcycle ready to go as soon as they get a hot tip! They sell their photographs to magazines for a high price.

Before You Begin

The drawing of the celebrity couple is built using two skeletons. Each skeleton is made up of a series of shapes, lines, and joints. Closely observe the direction the celebrities are looking in and the positioning of their shoulders, hips, knees, and feet. Note how the man is taller.

Step 1

Lightly draw a circle for the woman's head, followed by her chin and face cross. Sketch her neck and curved spine and an ellipse for her hips. Draw an oval for her chest with shoulders at an angle at the top. Sketch her bent arms, making sure the one on your left is shorter. Draw a guideline underneath. Sketch her front leg and then the shorter one crossing behind. Draw the man's skeleton in the same order. Note that his hand overlaps hers and his legs are apart.

Step 2

Shape the curved outlines of each person's form around the skeletons. Start drawing at their heads and work your way down to their feet. Pay attention to how her thigh and his arm are both hidden.

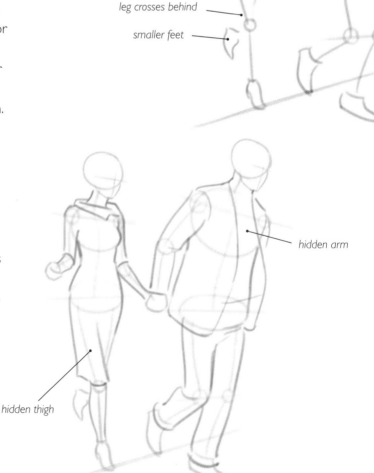

short forearm

overlapping hands

leg crosses behind

smaller feet

hidden arm

hidden thigh

fingers inside hand shape

square sunglasses

boxy bag

Step 3

Draw their facial features over the crosses. Sketch her sunglasses, nose, and mouth. Draw the outline of her hair around the top of her head. Follow the same order for his face and hair. Draw their fingers inside the hand shapes. Define their shoes and draw his collar, tie, and vest. Sketch her boxy bag over her wrist.

DRAWING TIP

Once you feel confident about drawing the structure of the human body, try drawing a person from a magazine or photograph using your new skills.

Step 4

Study how the light is hitting one side of their figures, creating darker shadowing on the other side of their bodies. With light pencil pressure, draw soft shading over the edges of their clothing, creating any gathering of fabric and shadows as you go. Add his buttons. Darken the shade of their shoes and hair, and her handbag. Create the outline of the photograph with a ruler. When you softly draw the faint angles of the streetscape in the background, your couple will be ready to dodge the paparazzi!

INTERESTING FACT → *US Weekly* reportedly shelled out $500,000 to print photos of Brad Pitt and Angelina Jolie strolling along a beach in Africa in 2005.

More Funky Things to Draw—Glitz & Glamour

MODEL MAKEUP

Professional makeup artists work in many areas of the fashion and movie industries. Makeup trends change every season and are created to complement certain fashion looks. A catwalk model can wear more outrageous and creative makeup styles, to accentuate a fashion designer's flamboyant creations. An actor's makeup is more classic and applied with precision. Colors and styles are chosen to complement the person's natural features.

Before You Begin

The snapshot of the model and makeup artist is based around several irregular shapes. The curved outlines of the figures are formed around these shapes. Observe how the model's face is constructed over a cross and her eyes are looking upward. Pay close attention to how both heads are cropped around the outside.

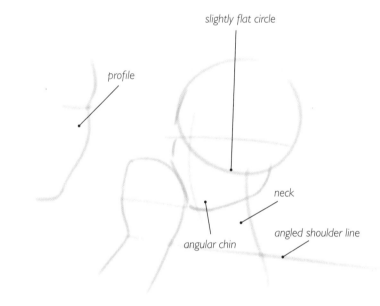

profile

slightly flat circle

neck

angular chin

angled shoulder line

Step 1

Lightly draw a slightly flattened circle for the model's head. Then draw an angular chin underneath. Sketch a face cross facing to your left. Sketch a line for the angle of the shoulders, and then draw the neckline. Draw a hand shape sitting against her chin and a curved line for the makeup artist's profile.

Step 2

Draw the hairline and profile of the makeup artist. Draw fingers inside the hand shape and develop the outline. Define the outline of the model's head and ear. Sketch soft curls around her forehead and define her neck. Sketch curved shoulders above the construction line. Draw a pencil in the artist's hand.

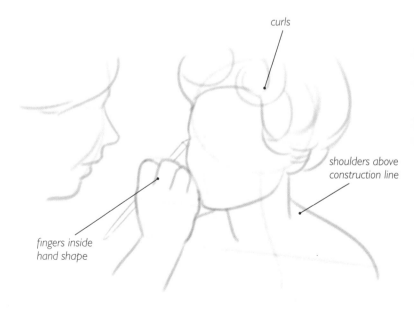

curls

shoulders above
construction line

fingers inside
hand shape

Step 3

Draw the model's eyebrows and eyes over the cross. Notice how she is looking up. Follow by drawing a curved nose and full mouth. Create the texture of her curls with a curved line pattern. Softly shade gray tone inside and around the curls and define her facial features. Once you add light shading across the skin and halter top, your model will be ready to face the camera!

DRAWING TIP

With a right-to-left drawing motion, practice your shading technique. Create light to dark gray tones using different pencil pressures with your pencil. Create a loose, open style of shading and more solid shades of gray.

INTERESTING FACT   → In ancient Mesopotamia, 5,000 years ago, women crushed up semi-precious stones to make cosmetics.

ROCK STAR ⭐ ⭐

Rock stars strut their stuff in front of large audiences, performing for their fans with brilliant musicianship and spectacular moves. True stars have talent, drive, and determination to succeed, and they firmly believe in themselves and their potential for greatness. With each new generation of music fans, another cool rock star arrives on the scene to be the next big thing.

Before You Begin

The rock star's form is built around a skeleton. To draw his pose correctly, observe the angles of all the body parts, especially the shoulders, chest, and legs. Notice where the rock star is facing and how his guitar is angled across his hips. Also, look at how the arm on your right wraps around the guitar neck.

Step 1

Lightly draw a head circle, adding a chin and tilted cross for the face. Draw a curved spine with shoulders at an angle. Sketch the chest circle and add the front bent arm. Draw the guitar on an opposing angle and draw the other arm wrapping around the guitar's neck. Sketch the straight and bent legs, paying attention to the feet. Draw the angled stage in the background.

Step 2

Draw the curved outline of the rock star's form around the skeleton. Start at the neck, working your way down to the feet. Observe how the forearm on your right is hidden behind the guitar.

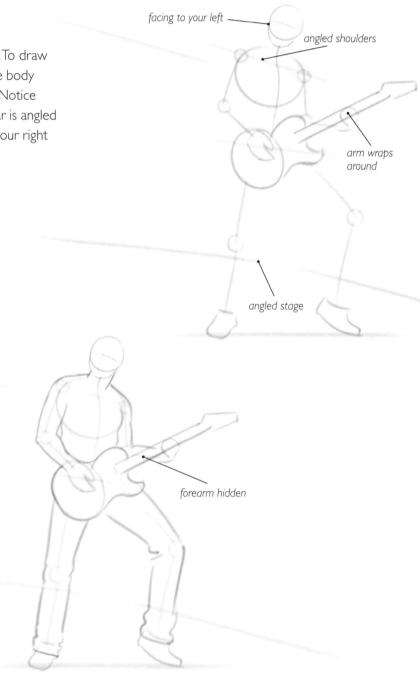

facing to your left

angled shoulders

arm wraps around

angled stage

forearm hidden

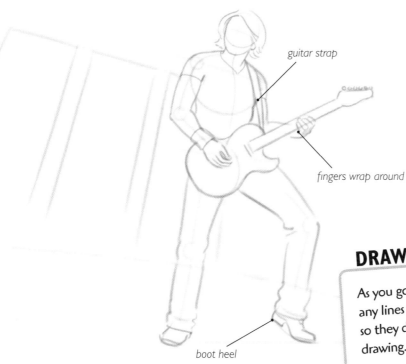

guitar strap

fingers wrap around

boot heel

Step 3

Draw hair around his head and add a "V" line for the neck of his t-shirt. Draw the t-shirt arms and the wristband. Draw fingers inside the hand shapes, paying attention to how the fingers wrap around the guitar's neck. Sketch the guitar strap and define his shoes, adding a boot-style heel. Lightly add detail to the stage.

DRAWING TIP

As you go, remember to erase any lines that you no longer need so they don't show in your final drawing.

Step 4

Starting with the eyes, draw facial features over the cross. Using light pencil pressure, shade highlights in his hair and build up shading over his figure. Pay special attention to the highlights on his jeans. Draw a necklace and add further detail to the guitar. Try adding fans either side of the stage. Once you add soft shadows across the stage, your rock star will be ready to rock!

INTERESTING FACT

→ The biggest rock star of all time was probably Elvis Presley. His style of "rock and roll" music changed the course of the music industry forever.

GLAMOUR JEWELRY

Well-known jewelry designers in Hollywood jump at the chance to adorn a Hollywood starlet headed to the Oscars. Jewels worn by famous actresses and models can be worth hundreds of thousands of dollars and are usually made from precious stones like diamonds, sapphires, rubies, and emeralds. Some women need a bodyguard to walk around with them to protect their valuable accessories! Glamour jewelry is chosen to complement gowns designed by world-renowned fashion designers like Chanel, Valentino, Galliano, and Versace.

Before You Begin

Your drawing of the woman wearing glamorous jewelry is based around a series of irregular shapes. To achieve the correct pose, you must draw the shoulders at the correct angle relative to the head and neck. The woman's form is drawn using shapes rather than a skeleton, so pay attention when adding the curves of her outline.

Step 1

Lightly draw the head shape, with a cross for the face looking to your left. Draw the neck at the same angle as the face. Lightly draw a guideline for shoulders at an angle underneath, with joints on each end. Next, sketch the rounded outline of the shoulders and the neckline of the dress.

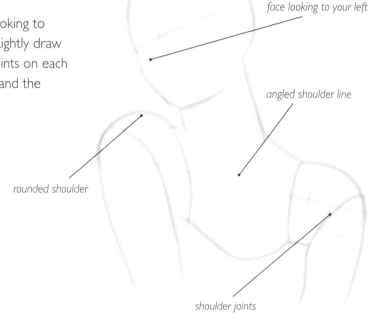

face looking to your left

angled shoulder line

rounded shoulder

shoulder joints

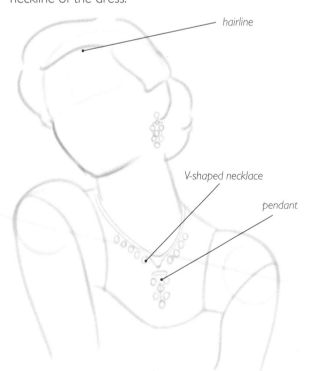

hairline

V-shaped necklace

pendant

Step 2

Sketch the woman's hairline around her forehead, followed by her ear. Draw the top outline of her hair around her head all the way down to the back of her neck. Draw her earring and sketch a V-shaped line for her necklace. Draw the pendant and the little jewels around the outline.

one eye larger

jewels defined

line pattern

jewels defined

Step 3

Draw eyes on either side of the cross; note that the eye on your right is larger. Follow with the nose and open mouth. Draw the details inside her ear. Define the outline of her form and her jewelry. Lightly draw a soft line pattern over her dress.

DRAWING TIP

Try sketching the model in this spread again, drawing your own style of earrings and necklace for her to wear!

Step 4

Define her eyes, drawing her pupils looking upward. For her hair, softly draw a line pattern to create texture. Using a light pencil pressure, shade medium gray highlights over her hair and light shading over her skin. Draw the second earring and shade soft highlights across her dress. Once you add further detail to her necklace and earring, the woman's jewelry will be ready to dazzle!

INTERESTING FACT → Inspired by the film *Titanic*, designer Harry Winston created a 15-carat blue diamond necklace that actress Gloria Stuart wore to the Oscars. Its estimated value is $20 million.

More Funky Things to Draw—Glitz & Glamour

MOVIE STAR ★★

Actors don't become famous overnight! Their journey to stardom and a life of glitz and glamour takes a lot of hard work and a little bit of luck. An actor goes to many auditions and plays many small roles before getting a big break. Once they are noticed for their talents and looks, their star begins to rise. Movie stars earn millions and can afford haute couture clothing created by the best fashion designers around the world.

Before You Begin

The drawing of the movie star is built around a skeleton and a dress shape. She is seen from a back view looking over her shoulder. The angle of her head, shoulders, and bottom are all the same. You must position her head correctly to achieve this pose. Observe where she is looking and how the spine is drawn.

Step 1

Lightly draw a circle for the head. Draw her pointed chin and cross for her face looking to your left. Sketch a curved spine from behind the chin. Draw a round chest with shoulders across the top. Sketch the outline of the bodice around the spine and then the skirt shape. Note how the hemline is rounded. Draw the bent arm on your right. Sketch the other arm and hand leaning against her bodice.

Step 2

Draw the outline of the movie star's body around the skeleton. Start with her neck and then draw her shoulders and arms. Observe how the line of her shoulder cuts across her neck. Draw her elbows and the fine, curved layers of fabric around the hem. Define the outline of her dress. Erase any lines you no longer need.

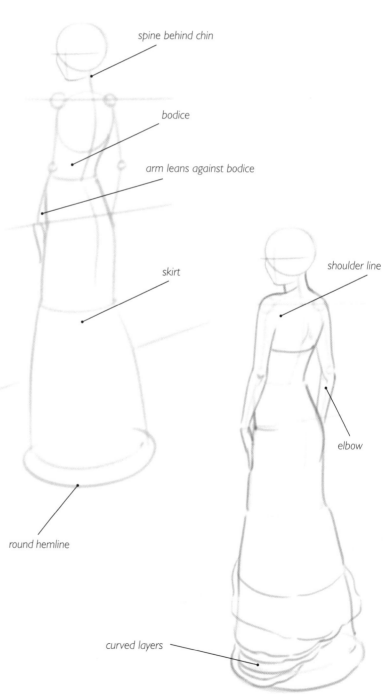

spine behind chin

bodice

arm leans against bodice

skirt

shoulder line

elbow

round hemline

curved layers

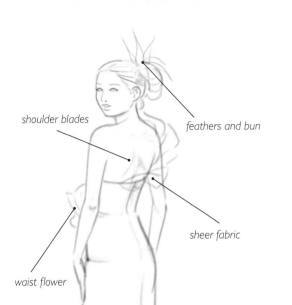

shoulder blades

feathers and bun

sheer fabric

waist flower

Step 3

Draw her facial features over the cross. Draw the eyes (one is smaller) and then the nose, mouth, and ear. Sketch her bun and the texture of her hair. Draw pointed feathers sticking up and curving over. Draw the faint, curved outline of the sheer fabric that folds over her shoulder onto her back. Softly shade her shoulder blades and the gathering that highlights her dress. Sketch her waist flower.

DRAWING TIP

When sketching something that has to be very lightly drawn, practice it on a separate piece of paper so you get your pencil pressure just right!

Step 4

Study how the different levels of shading make her hair and dress look shiny. Shade the darker texture of her hair and feathers. Darken and define her facial features. Use a light pencil pressure to softly shade her skin and the highlights and shadowing of her shiny dress. Note how it is darker around parts of the hem. Once you draw the paparazzi in the foreground, your movie star will be ready to strike a pose!

INTERESTING FACT

→ Some female celebrities such as Jennifer Lopez and Beyoncé like to have their photos taken from the back. This signature pose focuses on their elegant backs.

More Funky Things to Draw—Glitz & Glamour

RED CARPET ARRIVAL

Red carpet is used for special events like the Academy Awards, royal ceremonies, and welcoming important visitors from another country. In Hollywood, the red carpet arrival gives the paparazzi the opportunity to snap photographs of glamorous movie stars as they step out of their limousines wearing outfits created by top international designers. The next day, all the gossip columnists will be talking about who the stars arrived with and what they were wearing!

Before You Begin

The red carpet arrival is complex to draw because of the perspective of the limousine. It is at a sharp angle: bigger in the front of the picture and smaller in the distance. It is important that you draw the indicated guidelines first, as this will help you achieve the correct size and perspective.

Step 1

Lightly draw the top guidelines at an angle. Draw the bottom two guidelines a distance below. Observe how the guidelines come together in the distance. Draw the top and bottom of the limo, making sure they are drawn within the guidelines. Next, draw the smaller oval wheel and the larger round wheel. Sketch the door opening and red carpet lines.

Step 2

Draw the skeleton of the woman next, making sure the chest and hips line up with the guidelines. Observe how the head sits above the doorframe and the knees are at the same angle. Draw circles inside the wheels and then the outlines around them. Sketch the doorframe on the same angle as the red carpet and draw the limo's windows. Add the poles for the velvet rope.

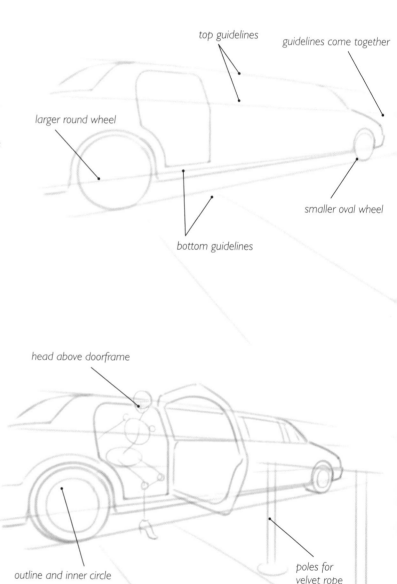

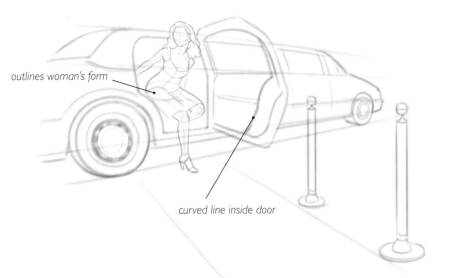

outlines woman's form

curved line inside door

Step 3

Draw the outline of the woman's form around the skeleton. Start at her head and work your way down her figure. Sketch the curved line inside the door. Add any other vertical and horizontal lines you see on the limo. Draw extra circles inside the wheels for the hubcaps. Define the poles along the red carpet.

DRAWING TIP

When you encounter a complex drawing, carefully study each step before you begin. Look at the different types of line and different sizes of the picture's elements.

Step 4

Draw the texture of the woman's hair, her facial features, and her necklace. Study the different levels of shading over the whole drawing. Using light pencil pressure, start at the top of the limo, shading light, medium, and dark gray tones over your picture. Add the rope between the poles. Once you shade them, your movie star will be ready to walk the red carpet!

INTERESTING FACT → The term "rolling out the red carpet" refers to making a special effort to display good hospitality.

More Funky Things to Draw—Glitz & Glamour

WALKING THE RED CARPET

Now that you have learned to draw a limousine and a movie star, combine the two drawings to create a full scene that captures the moment when celebrities arrive at an important event, like the Academy Awards. When a limousine drives up to the red carpet and the door opens, the paparazzi wait to see how famous the movie star is before they start taking photos. Once the stars begin to walk the red carpet, the paparazzi go crazy, snapping one picture after another. As the stars pose at the requests of photographers in their haute couture gowns, flashes can be seen sparkling in the air.

INTERESTING FACT → Movie stars wear gowns by fashion houses such as Versace and Chan when they go to the Academy Awards. Gianni Versace opened his fashion house in Milan in 1978. Coco Chanel was a pioneering fashion designer who began her fashion house in Paris in 1910.

DRAWING TIP

Before drawing the red carpet arrival scene, observe the perspective that the picture is drawn from. The angle of the red carpet is the most important element of this scene because it helps to determine the scale of the people. Study the paparazzi on the opposite side of the carpet. Look at how they are smaller and decrease in size as they disappear into the distance. When sketching this scene, draw the limo first, and then the red carpet. Follow with the movie star. Finally, draw the other people and the background.

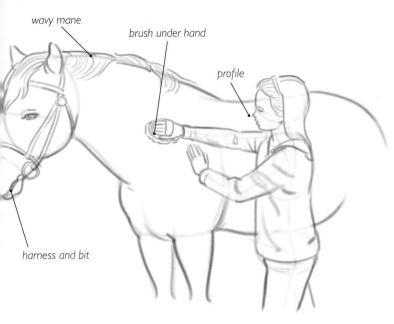

wavy mane

brush under hand

profile

harness and bit

Step 3

Draw the horse's fine wavy mane over the spine and head. Sketch an almond-shaped eye and add the nostril. Sketch the lines of the harness and bit around the horse's head. Draw the girl's profile, hair, and headband. Define the details of her clothing and draw fingers inside her hand shapes. Draw an oval brush with bristles under her right hand.

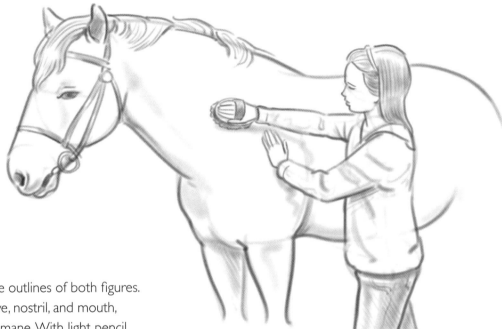

Step 4

Darken and define the outlines of both figures. Darken the horse's eye, nostril, and mouth, and the texture of its mane. With light pencil pressure, start at the top of the horse, adding the light to medium gray tones as you work downward. Do the same for the girl, paying attention to the texture of her hair. Your horse is now ready for grooming!

DRAWING TIP

"Irregular shapes" are shapes that look different when you turn them around, as opposed to symmetrical shapes like circles and squares that are the same on all sides. Irregular shapes look organic and natural.

INTERESTING FACT → Around 350 breeds of horses and ponies can be found throughout the world.

More Funky Things to Draw—Pony Club

PONY PULLING CART

For centuries, human beings have harnessed the power of the horse. Horsepower has provided power for engines in the manufacturing industry, transported goods and people, and developed social and sporting interests like equestrianism. Ponies are also used for many purposes such as pulling carts underground in mines and pulling plows for farmers. We should really be thankful for the important role these wonderful creatures have played in our history!

Before You Begin

This picture is complex. It has a number of stages, and the perspective is tricky. Take time to study all the stages of the drawing and see how the elements of the drawing connect.

Step 1

Lightly draw the pony's head, muzzle, and chest area. Draw its curved belly and rump. Sketch a guideline below the pony and draw its legs and feet sitting on the line. Make sure its back legs are crossed at the knees. Cross the horse's guideline with an angled guideline for the cart. Now sketch the rectangular backrest parallel to the cart guideline, followed by a thin shape for the seat. Draw the other rectangle below and a thin shape for the footrest. Sketch both wheels on the cart guideline, making sure the nearer wheel is bigger.

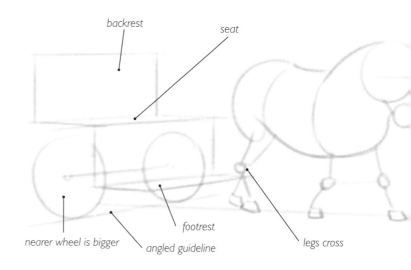

backrest

seat

nearer wheel is bigger

footrest

angled guideline

legs cross

Step 2

Draw the skeleton of the boy. Sketch the head, face cross, and spine. Draw a round chest, the arms, and solid thigh shapes resting flat on the seat. Sketch the bottom of the legs. Follow the same process for the girl, who is tall enough that her feet reach the footrest. Don't forget her hat.

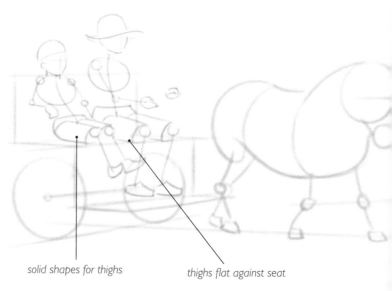

solid shapes for thighs

thighs flat against seat

backrest padding and bar   *spokes*   *traces*   *harness*

Step 3

Shape the details of the cart. Draw the padded backrest, the curved metal bar, and the traces and harness, and thicken the footrest. Create the tire and spokes for the front wheel. Thicken the back wheel. Starting at the pony's head, form its curved outline around the shapes. Do the same for the legs and draw a floppy mane. Sketch the details of its face and draw the bridle.

Step 4

Starting at the tops of the children's bodies, work your way down their figures, shaping their curved outlines around the skeletons. Draw the boy first and make sure you pay attention to the boy's overlapping feet and the girl's overlapping arms.

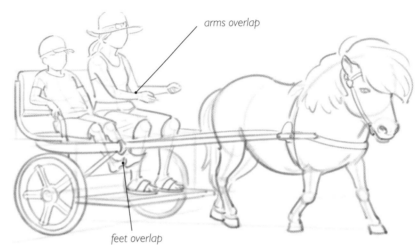

arms overlap

feet overlap

Step 5

Darken and define the outlines of the children and the horse. Draw the children's eyes, noses, and mouths over their face crosses. Define the details of their clothing and the details of the front wheel. Using light pencil pressure, shade light to medium gray tones over all figures. Add texture to the pony's mane and draw the reins in the girl's hands. Once you draw the grass below, your pony will begin to trot!

INTERESTING FACT

→ "Horsepower" is an internationally recognized unit of power. It is the amount of power needed to lift a weight of 165 pounds over a distance of 3 feet in 1 second.

More Funky Things to Draw—Pony Club

CROSS-COUNTRY ⭐⭐⭐

Cross-country equestrian jumping, often called just "cross-country," is a test of skill and endurance. During cross-country, a rider guides a horse to trot, gallop, and jump over a variety of obstacles in a set time frame. It is one of the few Olympic sports where men and women compete directly against one another. Eventing combines cross-country, dressage, and show jumping in an equestrian triathlon that only the most talented horses and riders can complete.

Before You Begin

The rider in this picture is constructed using a skeleton, and the horse is built using a series of irregular and rounded shapes. Construction lines and joints form the horse's legs. The most important elements of this drawing are the angle of the horse, its overlapping legs, and the positioning and angle of the rider.

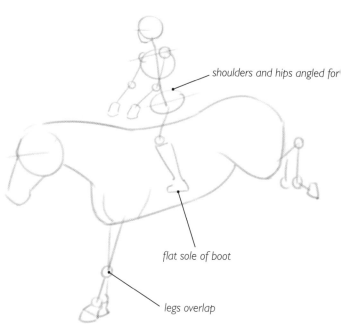

shoulders and hips angled for

flat sole of boot

legs overlap

Step 1

For the rider, lightly draw a round head with a pointed chin and add the spine. Draw a round chest and sketch the shoulders and hips, angled forward. Add the arms and legs. Pay attention to the flat sole of the boot. For the horse, draw a curved backbone and add a round head and a muzzle. Draw the neck, belly, and rump. Sketch the straight front legs, making sure they are crossed and floating above the line. Draw the bent back legs.

Step 2

Draw a guideline below the hooves. Starting at the head, shape the curved outline of the horse's form around the shapes. Work your way down its body until you get to the hind legs. Draw the hind leg in the front first and then the one hidden behind. Now add the flowing mane and tail and the eye. From the top, sketch the lines for the jump behind the horse.

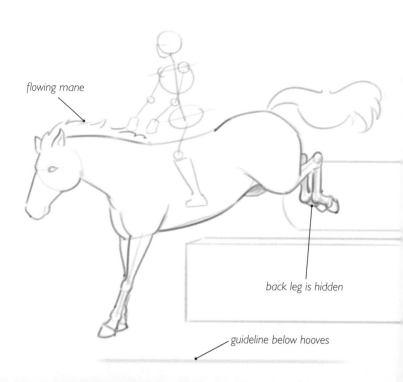

flowing mane

back leg is hidden

guideline below hooves

brim turned up

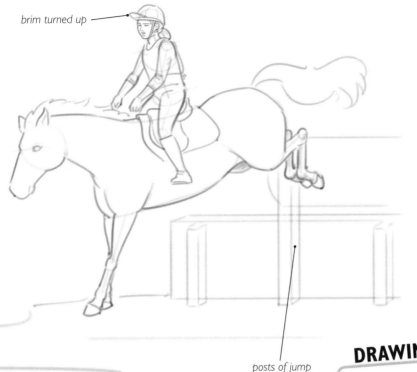

posts of jump

Step 3

Starting at the head, shape the outline of the rider's form around the skeleton. Draw the helmet with its upturned brim, and her hair and facial features. Work your way down, shaping the rider's clothing, gloves, and boot. Draw the saddle and saddle blanket. Sketch the three-dimensional posts of the jump and a wavy line for the water.

DRAWING TIP

An easy way to remember what horizontal means is to think of the horizon line at sunset!

Step 4

Draw the horse's bridle and reins. Sketch the girth under the saddle. With light pencil pressure, shade the texture of the horse's mane and tail. Shade light to medium gray tones over the rider and horse. For the jump, draw horizontal lines and shading for the wood. Once you add soft details and a reflection in the water, your horse will be ready to jump!

INTERESTING FACT → Cross-country was originally used by the military to test the stamina and courage of a horse over rough terrain.

More Funky Things to Draw—Pony Club

RIDING APPAREL

In the Middle Ages, horses and mounted knights wore armor into battle. After gunpowder was invented, balance and speed became more important than heavy armor, so riders started to wear jodhpurs, a style of pants adapted from India in the 1890s, or breeches. Clothing became more form-fitting to provide the rider and horse with greater comfort. Today's riders also wear helmets and boots carefully designed to keep them safe from injury.

Before You Begin

The drawing of the rider is built around a series of rounded and irregular shapes. The rider's body is fairly straight and she sits astride the horse's curved spine. Pay close attention to the angle of her shoulders and the way her head is turned.

Step 1

Lightly draw a curved line for the horse's spine. A distance above, sketch a round head with a chin and face cross looking to your left. Sketch a guideline for the shoulders. Then sketch the neck, shoulders, and shape of the jacket. Draw the bent front arm and the one behind. Sketch the overlapping hand shapes and the legs over the spine. Now draw a pointed riding boot.

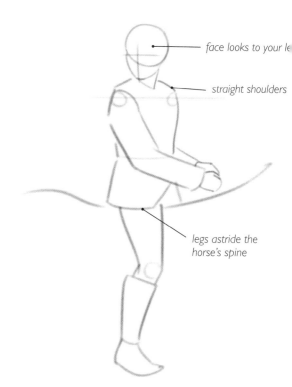

face looks to your le[ft]

straight shoulders

legs astride the horse's spine

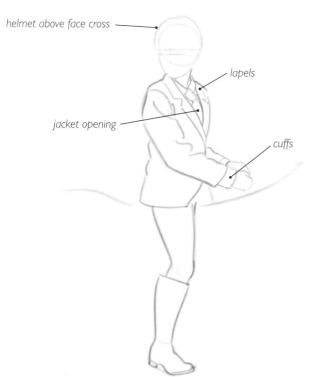

helmet above face cross

lapels

jacket opening

cuffs

Step 2

Draw a rounded helmet above the face cross. Sketch the jacket opening and lapels. Add a collar and tie. Create the folds of the sleeve and define the outline of her jacket, breeches, and boot. Don't forget the shirt cuffs.

strap over collar

flowing mane

saddle and blanket

girth

Step 3

Define the outline of the helmet. Add the rider's hair and ear, and the helmet strap over the collar. Define the rider's gloves. Draw a bumpy outline for the horse's mane and then draw the soft, flowing line work. Draw the outline of the saddle, saddle blanket, and girth.

DRAWING TIP

Once you feel confident drawing the rider, add a rider to the back of any horse you draw.

Step 4

Darken and define the outline of the rider and horse. Draw her eyes looking to your left and then draw her nose and mouth. Starting at her head, add light levels of gray tone as you work your way down to the horse. Pay attention to the folds in her jacket and sleeve. Once you add the soft pattern on the saddle blanket, your rider will be ready to compete!

INTERESTING FACT → From the 1600s to the early 1900s, female horseback riders commonly rode sidesaddle and wore an outfit called a riding habit, consisting of a long skirt, a tailored shirt and jacket, and a fancy hat.

More Funky Things to Draw—Pony Club

PONY RIDE ⭐⭐

Shetland ponies are good-tempered, gentle, and intelligent. They are a popular choice for rides at children's parties, fairs, and carnivals because of their size. Smaller children also ride them at horse shows and riding schools. However, they are also known for being impatient and uncooperative if they are not handled properly. Shetlands are a strong breed of pony and able to pull twice their own weight. It is not uncommon for a Shetland pony to live for 30 years!

Before You Begin

Both the pony and the child are built using rounded and irregular shapes. The pony's body looks like a barrel on its side. To achieve the correct pose for the pony, you must draw two baselines and line the skeleton legs up against them. For proper perspective, draw the pony's back legs shorter and thinner than its front legs.

Step 1

For the pony, lightly draw a barrel-shaped body that is flat on the bottom. Sketch four angled baselines underneath. Draw the skeleton legs with hooves lining up against the lines. Sketch the pony's neck at the top of the barrel and add a round head and muzzle. For the girl, draw a round head with the face cross and pointed chin looking to your right. Sketch her upper body and her leg hanging over the pony's side.

Step 2

Sketch the pony's pointed ears and add its bushy mane flopping over its head and neck. Shape the curved outline of its form, starting with the head and muzzle and going on to the body and legs.

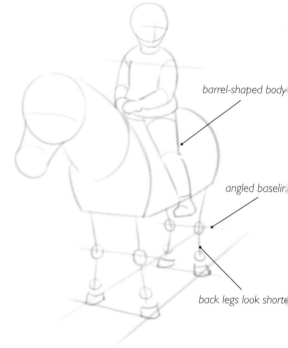

barrel-shaped body

angled baseline

back legs look shorter

bushy mane

braid

curved edge of helmet

Step 3

Draw the curved edge and rounded top of the girl's helmet. Shape her face and draw her braid. Draw her eyes, nose, and mouth over the face cross. Darken and define the details of her clothing and draw fingers inside the hand shapes. Now draw the saddle, saddle blanket, and girth.

DRAWING TIP

Don't be afraid to experiment with your own type of pencil strokes and marks. Be confident in developing your own style of drawing!

Step 4

Softly draw the curved fence next to the pony. Draw the pony's harness and curved straps. Add the stirrup around the girl's boot. With light pencil pressure, shade highlights in the pony's mane. Work your way down from the top of both figures, shading light to medium gray tones. Once you add the trees above and the shadowed grass below, your pony will be ready to ride!

INTERESTING FACT → Shetland ponies come from the Shetland Islands, 300 miles north of Scotland.

More Funky Things to Draw—Pony Club

GYMKHANA WINNER

Gymkhana was originally an Indian word for a sports arena. Now it's used to refer to a pony or horse show aimed at children. Riders show their skills in a variety of activities with the main focus being on having fun. Games are usually timed and also consist of speed pattern racing. Riders might have to weave in and out of poles, drop a potato in a bucket, step across overturned buckets, or balance a ball on a tennis racket.

Before You Begin

The gymkhana drawing is made up of irregular and rounded shapes. The most important aspect of this drawing is the angle of the rider and the horse. Notice that there is some foreshortening of the horse's body.

Step 1

For the horse, lightly draw a round head and a muzzle. Draw a curved backbone and outline of the chest, belly, and rump. Sketch two baselines below on an angle. Now draw the legs to meet the guidelines. For the rider, draw a round head with a face cross and add a pointed chin. Sketch the solid shapes of the rider's torso and bent front arm. Draw the other arm behind the horse. Sketch both legs with open feet against the guideline.

Step 2

Draw the curved outline of the horse's form around the shapes. Start by drawing the pointed ears and then define the head area. Form the legs and add the saddle that has three parts. Now draw a tail behind the horse's back legs.

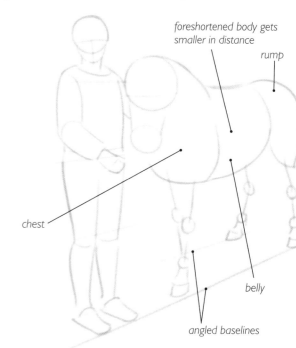

foreshortened body gets smaller in distance

rump

chest

belly

angled baselines

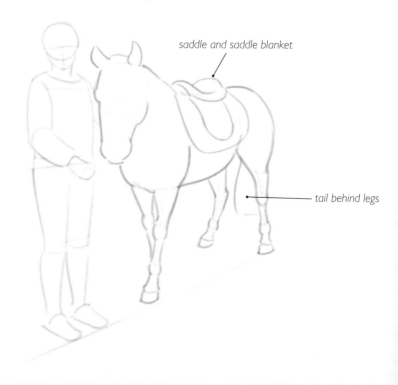

saddle and saddle blanket

tail behind legs

vest

winner's ribbon

Step 3

Draw the rider's eyes, nose, and mouth over the cross. Draw a rounded helmet with the strap under her chin. Sketch a collar and tie around her neck. Add a vest over her chest and then define other clothing details and her fingers inside the hand shape. Draw the horse's mane, eyes, and nostrils. Now sketch the winner's ribbon around its neck.

DRAWING TIP

When drawing a shadow, start off with a light pencil grip and build the darkness of the shadow gradually.

Step 4

Study the different levels of shading over both figures. Draw the horse's bridle and the details of the ribbon. Sketch the fine texture of the horse's mane and tail. Using light pencil pressure, shade light to medium gray tones over both figures from the top down. Once you draw the details of the arena in the background and the soft shadowing on the ground below, your horse will be ready to parade around!

INTERESTING FACT → Another term often used for this sort of competition is "o-mok-see," a Native American phrase meaning "riding big."

More Funky Things to Draw—Pony Club

RIDING TRAIL ★ ★ ★

Riding a horse through the woods is a popular way to learn horse management skills and feel a sense of adventure. It gives riders the opportunity to trot or gallop on trails and explore different aspects of a natural environment. Becoming familiar with a horse through the rugged terrain of the wilderness is a true bonding experience!

Observe that the whole picture is on an angle. To prepare for this drawing, turn your page horizontally (with the long edges at the top and bottom) and lightly sketch the angle of the trail. Next, draw both horses and riders in the foreground (front of the scene). Then sketch the two trees in the background, followed by the smaller horses and riders. With light pencil pressure, softly sketch the details of the trail, and the woods and ridge behind them.

DRAWING TIP

Now that you have learned to draw an array of different ponies and horses, you can apply your knowledge to sketching a larger scene.

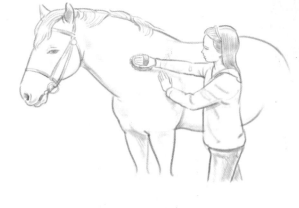

hinkler

Published by Hinkler Books Pty Ltd
45–55 Fairchild Street
Heatherton Victoria 3202 Australia
www.hinkler.com.au

© Hinkler Books Pty Ltd 2011

Design: Hinkler Design Studio
Typesetting: MPS Ltd
Prepress: Graphic Print Group
Illustrator: Paul Könye
Author: Kate Ashforth

ISBN: 978 1 7418 4050 6

Printed and bound in China

More Funky Things to Draw

Fairy Tales

Paul Könye ❀ **Kate Ashforth**

More Funky Things to Draw

Fairy Tales

INTRODUCTION

In Europe during the 18th and 19th century, old folk tales were reworked by authors like the Brothers Grimm and recorded in written form. These stories came to be known as fairy tales and allowed children the opportunity to escape into a world of fantasy. Fairy tales create an imaginary place far away filled with strange characters that are wicked, jolly, beautiful, and brave, where good always triumphs over evil.

THINGS YOU WILL NEED

- A gray lead pencil (HB or 2B).
- A pencil sharpener and a dish for shavings.
- Sheets of drawing paper.
- A clean eraser.
- Patience—learning drawing skills takes time and practice.
- Confidence—a positive attitude will help to develop your drawing skills!

Drawing Guidelines

1 There is a process in learning to draw. Follow the steps carefully and in order.
2 Always use light pencil pressure when beginning the first stage of a drawing.
3 If you feel unsure about the instructions, ask an adult for help.
4 Gray lead smudges easily. Pay attention to where your hand is on the page.
5 Clean the gray lead residue off your eraser by rubbing it against a spare piece of paper.
6 Most of the directions for drawing people don't mention the joints of the limbs or the hand and feet shapes, but they're still important! Be sure to draw them in.

Beginner Intermediate Expert

The stars at the top of each page grade the difficulty level of each drawing from beginner to intermediate or expert. Some drawings are trickier than others because of the level of detail, but if you carefully follow the basic principles of building a drawing from shapes and lines, you will learn to conquer both simple and complex drawings.

Follow the Steps

STEP I STEP 2 STEP 3 STEP 4

Throughout the following pages, you will find a variety of human subjects. To draw the human form, you need to construct a "skeleton" using a series of joints, lines, and shapes. The form of each subject is shaped around the skeleton using a curved outline. Study the shapes and joints that are drawn for the skeleton and the lengths of all the lines. Observe the line and curve of the spine and the positions and angles of all the body parts.

PENCIL TECHNIQUES FOR DRAWING 3-D FORMS

The boxes below show a variety of lines drawn for a subject.

irregular shapes   geometric shapes   3D shapes

When you arrive at each page of this book, observe the shapes drawn for each subject, and the way those shapes are angled.

To draw a three-dimensional form in the correct proportion, you must draw each shape at the correct size and angle. It is important to observe where the shapes are joined together to achieve a well-balanced drawing. You will also notice that leaving some areas white helps to highlight the form of your subject.

Shading and Pencil Pressure

Shading adds detail and definition to a subject. Apply different levels of shading with changes in pencil pressure—a light pencil grip creates a light gray tone, for example.

The boxes below show different levels of gray tone created by a pencil.

Light   Medium   Dark

More Funky Things to Draw—Fairy Tales

BEAUTY AND THE BEAST

The French tale of Beauty and the Beast is one of the best-known fairy tales around the world. Madame Gabrielle-Suzanne Barbot de Villeneuve first wrote the story as a novel for adults in 1740. Madame Jeanne-Marie Le Prince de Beaumont wrote the next version as a children's story in 1756. The heroine of this version is a woman seeking happiness, and she befriends a beast-like man who eventually turns into a prince. The appearance of the beast is not described in either story, so every artist can imagine him differently.

Before You Begin

The beauty is built around a skeleton and skirt shape, and the beast is constructed using a series of solid and rounded shapes. To achieve their correct poses, pay attention to the angles of the shoulders and front arms, and make sure that the crosses on their heads are facing each other.

Step 1

For the beauty, lightly draw a small round head with a pointed chin, looking to your right. Draw her spine, chest circle, and angled shoulders. Draw her hips and skirt shape. Sketch both of her arms. Then add two baselines below. For the beast, draw a large round head above the beauty's head with a solid chin shape facing to your left. Overlap his snout and then draw both characters' face crosses. Draw his solid chest and thick arms. Finish off the outline of his jacket.

Step 2

Work your way down from the beast's head, shaping the curved outline of his jacket. Pay attention to the cravat at his neck and his jacket cuff and frill. Shape the beauty's shoulders, neckline, arms, and bodice around the skeleton.

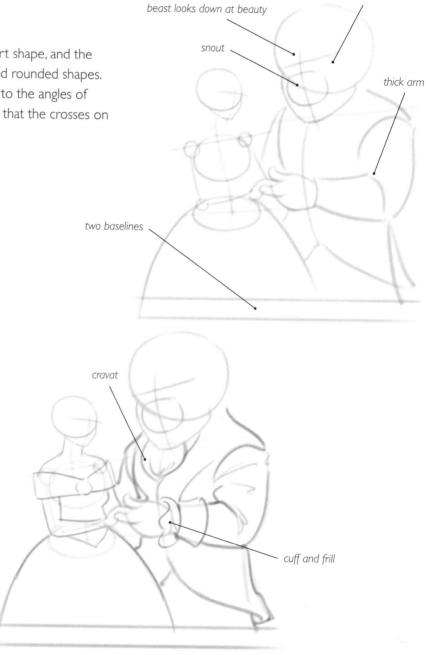

large head and shoulders

beast looks down at beauty

snout

thick arm

two baselines

cravat

cuff and frill

pointed ears

mane

bun

curly ponytail

gathered bodice

glove

Step 3

Draw the waves and curls of the beauty's hair around her head. Follow with her bun, ponytails and hair rosette. Add gathering and decoration to her neckline and define the glove. Draw the vertical lines of the balcony and extra horizontal lines below. Sketch the wavy mane of the beast flowing over the back of his head. Draw his pointed ears and then his eyes, snout, and open mouth over the cross. Develop the fine texture of his beard around his face. Define the extra details of his clothing.

DRAWING TIP

As you work through the steps of a drawing, remember to use a clean eraser to remove any lines you no longer need.

Step 4

Draw the beauty's eyes, nose, and mouth over the cross. Develop the beast's facial features, darkening his pupils and adding whiskers and fangs. With light pencil pressure, work your way down their figures, adding soft gray tone as you go. Darken and define their outlines. Once you add the sun shining above, your beauty and beast will be ready to fall in love!

INTERESTING FACT → Belle, the heroine's name in the traditional tale, means "beauty" in French.

FAIRY TALE CASTLE

Castles appear in many famous folk and fairy tales. The buildings themselves are towering palaces, often perched high in the mountains above the kingdom to protect its people from enemy attacks. Castles are made up of a number of elements: battlements surrounding the top of the castle, curtain walls, arrow slits, a donjon or tower, and a water-filled moat that circles the castle and is crossed via drawbridge. Other decorative details like spires and arched windows and doors accentuate a castle's magical design.

Before You Begin

The fairy tale castle is built around a series of block shapes and cylinders with cones on top. They are joined and stacked together to create different levels. The windows and pattern around the walls and towers give the castle its definition. Carefully study how light hits one side of the castle in step 4.

Step 1

Lightly draw the baseline at an angle. Sketch the central square shape with the angled shapes on either side. Sketch the three-dimensional block shape above the middle with a triangular roof on top. Draw the arch slightly off-center and add a wavy road.

Step 2

Sketch the tall cylinders with cone-shaped roofs on either side of the arch. Draw the shorter side cylinders on either side of the building. Sketch thinner cylinders above the walls, between the side and front towers. Add the rest of the cone-shaped roofs. Sketch the extra lines across the walls and a curved line inside the arch.

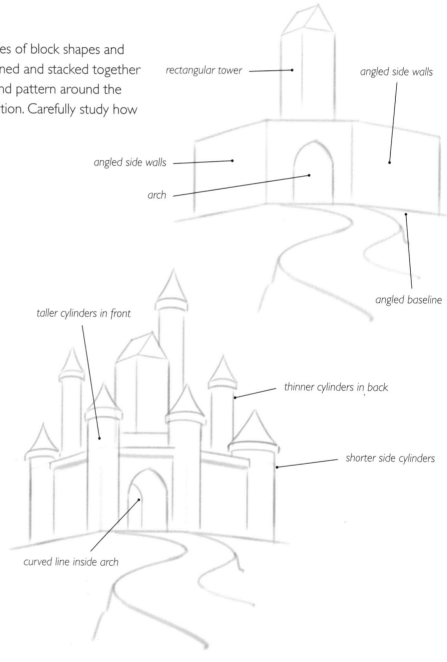

rectangular tower

angled side walls

angled side walls

arch

angled baseline

taller cylinders in front

thinner cylinders in back

shorter side cylinders

curved line inside arch

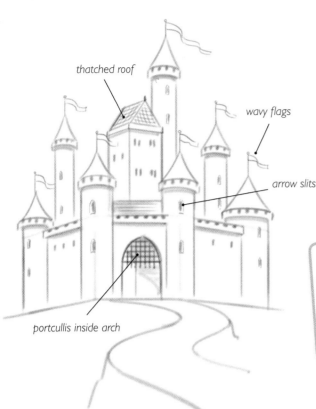

thatched roof

wavy flags

arrow slits

portcullis inside arch

Step 3

Draw all of the thin arrow slits first. Sketch the patterned detail around the top of the walls and towers and add all of the wavy flags. Add the thatched roof and the portcullis gate inside the arch.

DRAWING TIP

Look for pictures of some other fairy tale castles and try adding different design elements to your drawing.

Step 4

Study the different levels of gray tone over the castle and observe how the light hits one side of the building. With light pencil pressure, start at the rooftops and softly shade until you reach the base. Pay attention to the shadows inside the door arch and around the towers and walls. Once you add fir trees and rocky details in the foreground, your castle will then turn into a kingdom!

INTERESTING FACT → The earliest known castle was built in Gomdan, Yemen, over 2,000 years ago.

SNOW WHITE ⭐ ⭐ ⭐

The tale of Snow White comes from Germany. Snow White is a princess who is so beautiful that her stepmother becomes very jealous and tries to have her killed. Snow White runs away and hides in a cottage that turns out to belong to seven dwarfs. They help to protect her from the evil queen's schemes. The first written accounts of this old story came from the Brothers Grimm in the early 1800s. There are similar tales from Italy, Greece, Albania, and Scotland.

Before You Begin

Snow White and the dwarfs are built around a series of rounded shapes and lines. To achieve the correct poses, study the angles of all of Snow White's body parts and the dwarfs' heads and feet. You will observe that all of their heads are in line. Also, study how their faces are drawn over the crosses.

Step 1

Lightly draw Snow White's round head with a pointed chin looking to your left. Sketch the dwarfs' heads on either side and then draw all of the facial crosses. Sketch the top part of Snow White's skeleton, paying attention to the angled shoulders and hips. Draw her parallel bent legs. Sketch the round bodies of the dwarfs. Add the arms and legs, making sure their feet are below her body.

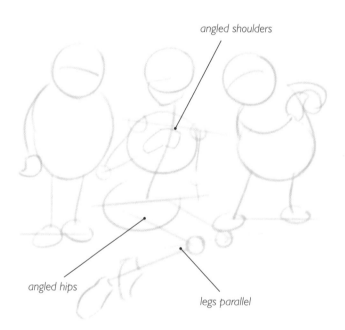

angled shoulders

angled hips

legs parallel

hair

open fingers

folds in skirt fabric

Step 2

Shape the outline of Snow White's form around the skeleton. Start at her hair and work your way down to her feet. Pay attention to the open fingers inside the hand shape and the way the fabric folds around her legs.

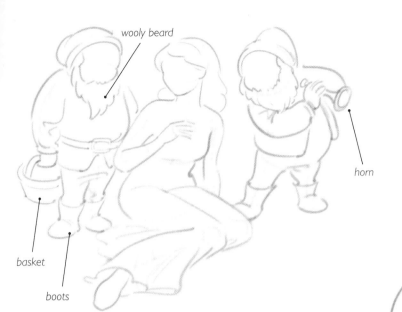

wooly beard

horn

basket

boots

Step 3

Shape the outlines of the dwarfs' bodies. Start with their hats and then add their woolly beards. Shape the curved outlines of their jackets and form their legs and boots. Define their hands then add the horn and basket.

hand and flower

checked pattern

Step 4

Darken and define their curved outlines. Draw their facial features over the crosses. Sketch the eyes first, then the nose and mouth. Add a checked pattern and flowers to the dwarf's basket and give him another hand that is holding a flower. Define his belt. Define the details of Snow White's bodice and add a buckle to her shoe. Give Snow White a hair ribbon and define her neckline and sleeves.

Step 5

Define Snow White's facial features. Using light pencil pressure, shade soft gray highlights over all of the figures. Start at their heads and work your way down. Once you add detail to the ground and the forest in the background, your characters will be ready to become friends!

INTERESTING FACT ➞ The film *Snow White and the Seven Dwarfs* was the first full-length animated feature made by Walt Disney. Hardly anyone believed it would be a success when it debuted in 1937, but the film sold out across America.

EVIL QUEEN ★ ★ ★

One of the most memorable evil queens of all fairy tales is Snow White's stepmother. She is driven into a rage when Snow White's beauty begins to outshine her own. The evil queen in Walt Disney's classic animation of the fairy tale says, "Mirror, mirror, on the wall, who is the fairest of them all?" The evil queen is so jealous of Snow White's beautiful looks that she feeds the girl a poisoned apple!

Before You Begin

Carefully study each stage of the drawing process. The evil queen's throne is three-dimensional and her figure is drawn over the top. The throne is constructed with a box shape for the base and a flatter curved headboard at the back. The queen is built around a skeleton and a skirt shape.

Step 1

Lightly draw the guidelines and the baselines. Draw the vertical lines of the box shape within the baselines. Sketch the short parallel lines at the top and base of the box. Add two lines on the front of the box and the curved headboard behind the box.

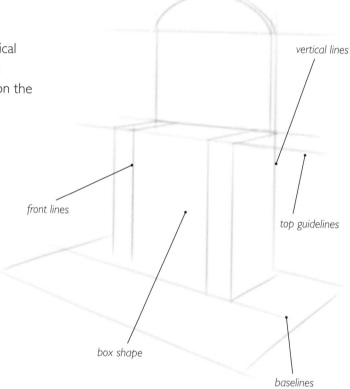

vertical lines

front lines

top guidelines

box shape

baselines

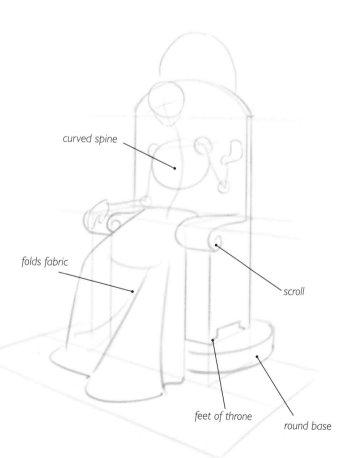

curved spine

folds fabric

scroll

feet of throne

round base

Step 2

Draw the side of the throne on your right. Draw the arms of the throne, including the scrolls. Form the form of the throne inside the box. Sketch the round base underneath. Draw the top of the evil queen's skeleton with a curved spine, and add her face cross. Draw her skirt shape inside the box shape with the folds of fabric sitting in front. Add a half-circle to the top of the throne.

collar

foreshortened arm

cape

hemline

Step 3

Work your way down from the queen's neck, shaping her curved outline around the skeleton. Pay attention to the foreshortening of the bent arm. Draw fingers inside the hand shapes. Add her pointed collar and curved neckline. Define the cape that runs down to her skirt and draw the hemline. Create the floor and folds of the curtain behind the throne. Don't forget the apple.

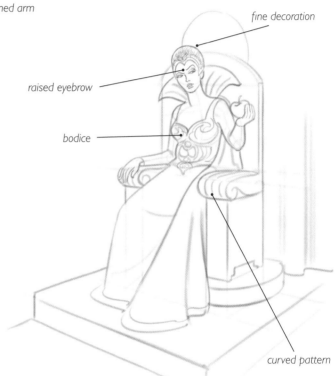

fine decoration

raised eyebrow

bodice

curved pattern

Step 4

Draw the queen's facial features over the cross. Sketch her eyes looking to your right, followed by the nose and open mouth. Draw one eyebrow up and the other one down. Sketch the fine details of her headpiece and the line patterns on the throne and her collar. Add the pattern to her bodice.

Step 5

With light pencil pressure, add the soft patterns to the half-circle and the bottom of the throne. Darken and define the queen's outline. Work your way down from her head, adding light levels of shading. Now your queen is ready to reign!

INTERESTING FACT → Lucille LaVerne created the powerful voice for the evil queen in Disney's *Snow White and the Seven Dwarfs*. She also did the voice for the old hag character. To achieve the difference, she removed her false teeth!

More Funky Things to Draw—Fairy Tales

CINDERELLA ★ ★

Cinderella is a kind young woman who lives in difficult circumstances until a magical guardian helps her to find happiness. The story of Cinderella has appeared in many forms in different cultures around the world. The earliest version comes from China and was written down by Tuan Ch'eng-shih in the 9th century. A Frenchman named Charles Perrault wrote down the next version of the fairy tale in 1697. He introduced elements such as the pumpkin carriage, animal servants, and the famous glass slipper.

Before You Begin

Cinderella is drawn around a skeleton and a bell-shaped skirt. You will observe that her body is angled to make her appear to be running down the stairs. To achieve the correct pose, pay close attention to the angles of her head and spine, and her arms. Also, note how the stairs are thinner at the top and become thicker toward the bottom.

Step 1

Lightly draw a round head. Add a pointed chin and face cross looking to your left. Sketch a spine and chest circle at an angle. Draw tilted shoulders with bent arms and open hand shapes. Add a bell-shaped skirt with an overskirt and a fabric train that looks like the top of a heart. Connect the skirt to the hand on your right. Sketch the lines of the banister. Don't forget the shoeless foot.

Step 2

Draw the curve and bottom piece of the banister, and add lines to give it form. Shape the top half of Cinderella's body around the skeleton. Draw the jagged outline of the stairs, which are shallow at the top and taller at the bottom. Create a wavy hem for the skirt and add the folds.

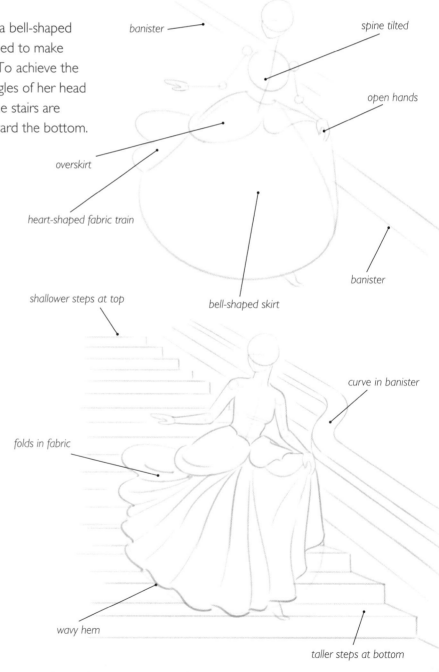

banister

spine tilted

open hands

overskirt

heart-shaped fabric train

banister

shallower steps at top

bell-shaped skirt

curve in banister

folds in fabric

wavy hem

taller steps at bottom

smallest post

bun

slipper

ringlet

cap sleeves

largest post

Step 3

Draw the vertical posts of the banister from smallest to largest. Sketch Cinderella's elegant hairstyle with a ringlet under the bun. Draw her eyes, nose, and mouth over the face cross. Sketch soft, puffy cap sleeves and define the bodice of her gown. Define her fine fingers and add a tiny glass slipper in the background.

DRAWING TIP

Staircases can be difficult to draw. Practice drawing a staircase separately before you start your picture.

Step 4

Darken and define her outline and her facial features. Using light pencil pressure, shade the soft texture of her hair and add an earring. Work your way down the picture, shading light gray highlights over her figure. Once you add the shadows on the staircase, Cinderella will be ready to escape at midnight!

INTERESTING FACT → The Walt Disney animation of *Cinderella* was adapted from the Charles Perrault story and appeared in theaters in 1950. Even back then, the film cost several million dollars to produce!

More Funky Things to Draw—Fairy Tales

PRINCE ★ ★ ★

There are many fairy tales in which a prince appears to aid the heroine. These princely characters are handsome and heroic men who will do anything to help a woman escape her desperate situation. The prince of a traditional fairy tale usually has romantic intentions and falls in love with the heroine of the story. After his kindness wins her heart, they marry and live happily ever after.

Before You Begin

The prince is built around a skeleton. His horse is constructed using a series of rounded shapes and skeleton legs. When drawing the horse, pay close attention to the angle of its spine and the positioning of its chest circle and legs. Observe that the prince's hips seem to disappear behind the horse's spine.

Step 1

Lightly draw the prince's rounded head with a pointed chin looking to your right. Draw his curved spine and chest and add a line for eyes. Sketch a bent arm pointing up and half of the other arm. For the horse, sketch a round head, and then add a snout and a line for eyes. Draw a curved spine underneath the prince and add the horse's neck and chest circle. Sketch the horse's belly and hind legs at an angle. Draw the front leg followed by the leg behind. Draw the prince's hips over the horse's spine. Now add his leg dangling over the horse.

Step 2

Shape the outline of the prince's form around the skeleton. Start at the head, drawing his wavy hair, profile, and ear. Add a pointed collar and the top of his cape. Then shape his tunic and belt. Sketch the top of his leg and form the boot. Outline the saddle. Erase any lines you no longer need.

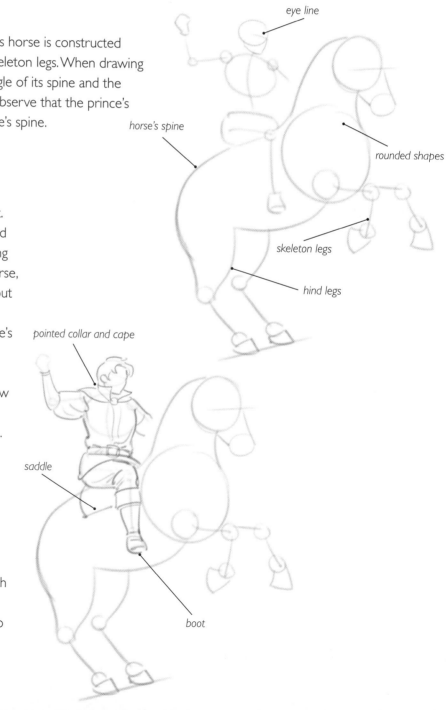

eye line

horse's spine

rounded shapes

skeleton legs

hind legs

pointed collar and cape

saddle

boot

mane

flowing cape

girth

puffy tail

Step 3

Draw fingers inside the hand shape and a sword pointing backward. Continue the flowing and wavy cape from the shoulders. Shape the curved outline of the horse's form around the skeleton. Start at the head, drawing the pointed ears and snout area. Sketch the puffy mane and tail then shape the muscular legs and hooves. Now add the girth (the strap that holds the saddle on).

DRAWING TIP

Texture is the look and feel of a surface. Different types of pencil marks are repeated to create texture.

Step 4

Sketch the eyes of the prince and the horse over the eye lines. Sketch the prince's nose, mouth, and ear. With light pencil pressure, draw a fine line pattern to create the texture of the horse's mane and tail. Sketch the line work of the harness. Work your way down from the top of the figures, adding soft levels of gray tone to highlight their forms. Now your prince is ready to meet his princess!

INTERESTING FACT → One of the most famous English warriors of the Middle Ages (the 1300s) was Edward the Black Prince. He was given this title because he wore black armor in battle.

More Funky Things to Draw—Fairy Tales

THE PRINCESS AND THE PEA

This fairy tale was first written down by Danish author Hans Christian Andersen in 1835. A prince looking for a bride meets many princesses, but they all have flaws. One rainy night, a lady appears at the palace gates claiming to be a princess. They give her a bed with one tiny pea hidden beneath 20 mattresses, thinking that only a real princess would be able to feel it. The next morning she complains of a lump in the bed, so the prince asks her to marry him!

Before You Begin

The drawing of the princess and the pea is built around a three-dimensional rectangle shape. There are three bedposts and 20 mattresses. Pay attention to the thickness of the bedposts and the angle of the rectangular box shape. Also, notice how the inside of the canopy is drawn in parallel with the mattresses.

Step 1

For the box shape, lightly draw the long side of the base and then the short side. Draw all three vertical lines, paying attention to the different heights. Sketch the top of the box and the two lines underneath.

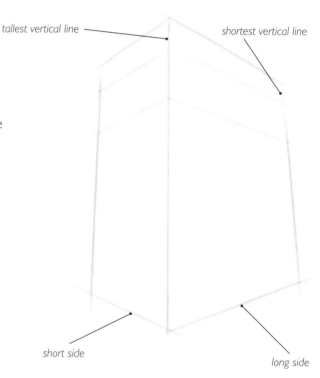

tallest vertical line

shortest vertical line

short side

long side

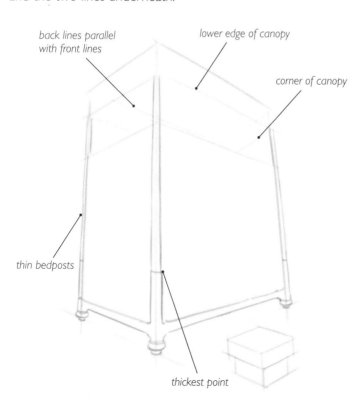

back lines parallel with front lines

lower edge of canopy

corner of canopy

thin bedposts

thickest point

Step 2

Define and thicken the bedposts up to the second line at the top, the lower edge of the canopy. Thicken the base and add the three rounded feet. Draw two lines underneath the bed top that are parallel with the front mattress lines. Add the right-hand corner of the canopy at an angle. Sketch the top of the table on the floor in the shape of a diamond. Then add the sides and lightly draw the smaller box shape underneath.

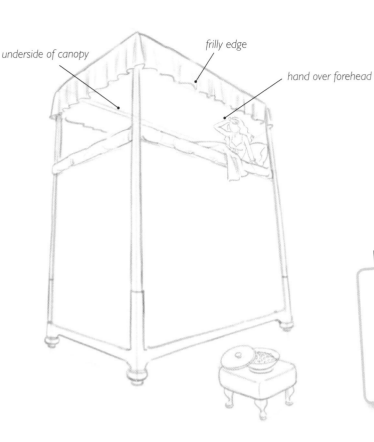

underside of canopy

frilly edge

hand over forehead

Step 3

Draw the frilly outline of the canopy and define its underside. Create the top mattress and sketch the princess with her hand over her forehead. Define the shape of the small table and add the bowl of peas. Lightly shade the vertical folds of the canopy.

DRAWING TIP

Don't be afraid to add imaginative elements and detail to your drawing as you go. Try developing your own background that includes other characters.

Step 4

Starting at the bottom, sketch the irregular lines of the mattresses. Remember there are 20 in total. With a sharp pencil, create the features of the princess's face and body, and add a fine pattern to the bedposts. Using light pencil pressure, add soft shading under the canopy and bed base. Once you shade and define the table and peas in the foreground, your princess will be ready to sense the pea!

INTERESTING FACT

→ Andersen wrote many famous fairy tales, including *The Ugly Duckling*, *The Emperor's New Clothes*, and *Thumbelina*.

FAIRY GODMOTHER

Wouldn't it be wonderful to have someone to help you sort out your problems and make your wishes come true? In fairy tales, fairy godmothers care for the hero or heroine of the story. They guide their protégés by sharing their wisdom, and use magical powers to help change their fortunes. Fairy godmothers usually appear in stories when the hero or heroine feels most downtrodden. They bring an element of hope to a story.

Before You Begin

The fairy godmother's figure is made up of a skeleton on the top half and a rounded bell shape for her skirt. To achieve her correct pose, you must draw the two guidelines that help you position her shoulders and hips, and bent arms and open hands. Also, closely follow the changes in her gown between each step and the many folds and details added to the fabric.

Step 1

Lightly draw the fairy godmother's round head with a chin pointing to your left. Draw a spine behind the chin and a cross for her facial features. Sketch two guidelines for shoulders and hips. Sketch a rounded bell-shaped skirt. Draw an oval for the chest and bent arms on either side with open hand shapes.

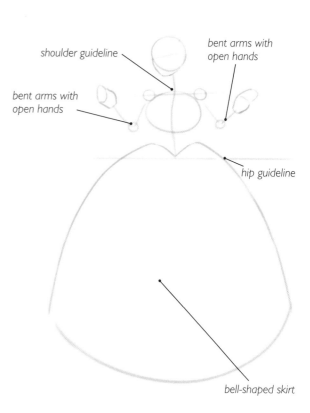

shoulder guideline

bent arms with open hands

bent arms with open hands

hip guideline

bell-shaped skirt

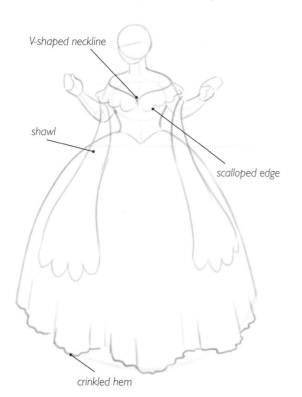

V-shaped neckline

shawl

scalloped edge

crinkled hem

Step 2

To draw the top half of the fairy godmother's body, shape her curved outline around the skeleton. Observe how the V-shaped neckline with a scalloped edge is drawn across her chest. Sketch the shawl draping over her bent elbows and skirt. Draw the crinkled edge of her hem around the base of the skirt and add folds in the fabric.

cloud-shaped hair

choker

wider folds

thinner folds

Step 3

Sketch a crown over the top of her head and add cloud-shaped hair hanging around her face. Shape the outline of her face and draw her eyes, nose, and mouth over the cross. Sketch her fingers inside the hand shapes and add the extra detail to her neck, chest, and waist. Draw lines running down her shawl and the folds of her skirt: wider at the top, thinner at the bottom. Sketch the thinner folds down her skirt and draw her wand and choker-style necklace.

DRAWING TIP

When drawing very light patterns and details, imagine your pencil is a feather so you don't grip it too tightly.

Step 4

Using light pencil pressure, gently draw the fine patterns on her crown, neckline, and shawl. Shade a wavy texture for her hair and add rosettes to her choker and neckline. Softly shade her skin and define her face and wand. Work your way down her dress, adding light gray tone to her waist and alongside the folds in her gown. Once you add a darker shadow under the neckline and skirt, your fairy godmother will be ready to grant wishes!

INTERESTING FACT → In the Disney film *The Princess and the Frog*, the blind fairy godmother, Bayou, is 197 years old!

KNIGHT IN SHINING ARMOR

In fairy tales, a knight in shining armor is a character who arrives to save a damsel in distress. He wields a sword and rides in gallantly on his horse. He serves his king or lord and lives to guard and protect the kingdom's castle. This virtuous knight also roams the kingdom engaging in heroic acts and displaying courtesy, courage, and honor. A knight in shining armor is taught to respect women and be devoted to the service of a lady.

Before You Begin

The knight is built around a skeleton. He is seen from the side with one leg extended and the other foot up on a wall. To achieve the correct pose, you must carefully observe how his legs extend from the hips and where his feet are placed. For the final step, study the different levels of gray tone and the areas that are left white.

Step 1

Lightly draw a round head with a pointed chin facing to your left. Then add the eye line. Draw the spine, chest circle, and tilted hips. Sketch the bent arm and the top part of the other arm. Draw three converging lines beneath the hips and add the toe lines that run across. Draw the bent leg with foot on the wall and the straight leg stretching to the ground.

Step 2

Build the form of the knight around the skeleton. Starting at the head and working your way down, draw the curved outline of his torso. Then add the angled shield. Pay attention to the pointed outline of his spaulders (shoulder plates). Sketch the thighs and greaves (shin armor).

Step 3

Draw the side-on profile of the knight. Sketch an ear behind his chin and shape the curved lines of his hair and ponytail. Add a curved line pattern around his spaulders and a small shield on his chest. Draw his belt, and his surcoat draping over his legs. Sketch his vambrace (forearm armor) and define the greaves and boots. Draw the sword and wrap his fingers around the hilt. Don't forget the inner line shaping the shield.

fingers wrap around hilt

vambrace

belt

surcoat

DRAWING TIP

When shading with a gray lead, apply softer shading first and build it up to a darker gray tone if needed. If you are shading a vertical area, turn your page sideways so you can use horizontal strokes.

Step 4

Sketch the knight's mouth and eye. With light pencil pressure, softly feather his beard and hair. Darken and define his outline. Observe how light is hitting the armor. Starting at the sword, softly apply various levels of shading over his whole figure. Once you add the design to his shield and softly define the bricks below, your knight will be ready to rescue his damsel!

INTERESTING FACT → A woman might say "You are my knight in shining armor!" to describe someone courageous who has saved her from a situation she dislikes.

More Funky Things to Draw—Fairy Tales

THE FROG PRINCE

The Brothers Grimm wrote down the story of the Frog Prince in Germany in 1812. When a young princess drops her favorite golden ball into a pond, a frog offers to retrieve it if she promises to take him home and care for him. She takes the ball and runs away, but the frog follows her and the king makes her keep her promise. She feeds the frog and allows him to sleep in her bed. After three nights, the frog's enchantment wears off and he becomes a handsome prince!

Before You Begin

The princess is drawn using a series of solid shapes. The positioning of the head, shoulders, hips, and arms is very important. Two guidelines will help you draw her body at the right angle. Her bent arm hides her shoulder and the frog sits on her flat and outstretched hand.

Step 1

Lightly draw a rounded head. Sketch a pointed chin looking to your right and a line for eyes. Draw the neck at an angle, followed by the curved lines of the arm on your left. Lightly sketch the angled guidelines and draw the rest of the torso. Draw the other shoulder partly behind the neck with the forearm leaning against the body. Sketch the flat outstretched hand.

Step 2

Shape the curved outline of the hair around the princess's head. Sketch her profile and ear. Then draw the tiara curving over her head. Work your way down, shaping the curved neckline of her dress and puffy sleeve. Draw the frog in her hand and the heart-shaped frame.

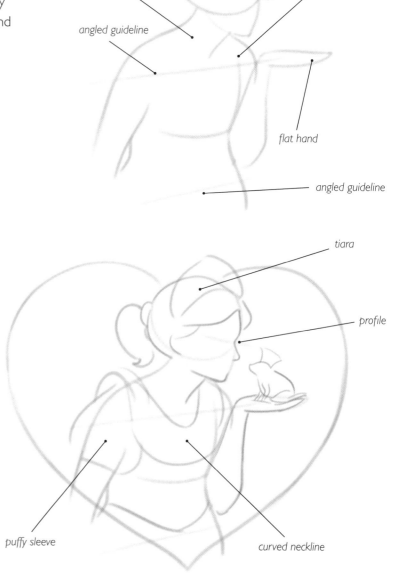

neck bent forward

shoulder behind neck

angled guideline

flat hand

angled guideline

tiara

profile

puffy sleeve

curved neckline

Step 3

Draw the fine details of the tiara. Add wavy lines for hair texture and define her eyes, nose, mouth, ear, and earring. Create the crinkled edge and folds of the ruffles inside the shapes of her dress. Further define her puffy sleeve and add line patterns to her waist area. Define the details of the frog.

ruffled neckline

line pattern

Step 4

Darken and define the outline of the princess. With light pencil pressure, work your way down both figures, shading the different levels of gray tone. Observe how some areas are left white to create highlights. Add circular jewels inside the tiara. Once you add the soft details of the pond behind, your princess will be ready to kiss the frog!

DRAWING TIP

To keep your picture from smudging, try turning your drawing around as you go to reach different parts of your picture.

INTERESTING FACT → In some interpretations of the story, the frog persuades the princess to kiss him, which breaks the spell.

More Funky Things to Draw

Cute Critters

Paul Könye ❀ **Kate Ashforth**

Cute
Critters

More Funky Things to Draw

Cute Critters

INTRODUCTION

From koalas in Australia to pandas in China, every country has its share of cute critters that are loved for their fluffy fur, big eyes, or awkward movements. They are the subjects of illustrations, clothing, and home décor because of their continuing popularity. Since they are so easy to characterize, they are also a favorite theme in cartoons and movies.

THINGS YOU WILL NEED

- A gray lead pencil (HB or 2B).
- A pencil sharpener and a dish for shavings.
- Sheets of drawing paper.
- A clean eraser.
- Patience—learning drawing skills takes time and practice.
- Confidence—a positive attitude will help develop your drawing skills!

Drawing Guidelines

1 There is a process in learning to draw. Follow the steps carefully and in order.
2 Always use light pencil pressure when beginning the first stage of a drawing.
3 If you feel unsure about the instructions, ask an adult for help.
4 Gray lead smudges easily. Pay attention to where your hand is on the page.
5 Clean the gray lead residue off your eraser by rubbing it against a spare piece of paper.

Beginner   Intermediate   Expert

The stars at the top of each page grade the difficulty level of each drawing from beginner to intermediate or expert. Some drawings are trickier than others because of the level of detail, but if you carefully follow the basic principles of building a drawing from shapes and lines, you will learn to conquer both simple and complex drawings.

Follow the Steps

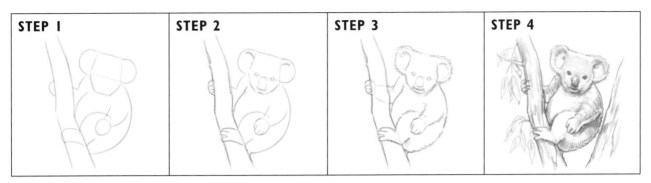

Study the changes between each step and the pencil techniques used. You will notice that the animals are drawn using a series of rounded and irregular shapes and different types of line. Fur and shading are applied in the final steps.

PENCIL TECHNIQUES FOR DRAWING FUR

The boxes below show three types of pencil work used for drawing fur.

| striped fur | long soft fur | fine fur |

Observe the types of marks that are applied for the texture of fur. Are they thick, wavy, or fine? Are they soft, darker, and more defined? These differences are achieved with changes in the pressure and direction of your pencil strokes.

Various pencil marks create the look and feel of a subject's fur. Begin by shaping the outline of each subject with the types of marks you see in the steps. Then work your way inward, applying steady and even pencil strokes. Softer fur textures require a blunter pencil and darker, defined pencil marks require a sharper pencil.

Shading and Pencil Pressure

Shading adds detail and definition to a subject. Apply different levels of shading with changes in pencil pressure—a light pencil grip creates a light-gray tone, for example.

The boxes below show different levels of gray tone created by a change in pencil pressure.

Light   Medium   Dark

More Funky Things to Draw—Cute Critters

PUPPY ★ ★

Puppies may not be able to open their eyes at birth, but they have a fully functional sense of smell. They are fully dependent on their mothers in the first few weeks of life and become distressed if they are separated from their brothers and sisters. At around four weeks of age, puppies begin to bark, growl, bite, and wag their tails. Their coordination develops rapidly and their strength improves as they begin to spar with their siblings and discover the world outside.

Before You Begin

Study the changes between each step before you start. You'll see that the back legs of the puppy don't need to be drawn because they are hiding behind the grass in the final step. The most important thing is to achieve the correct angle so you see the puppy from the right perspective. Also observe the angles and shapes of the body, limbs, and head.

Step 1

Lightly draw the geometric head shape on a slight angle with a snout. Next, draw a backbone then follow with the outline of the belly. Sketch leg shapes that are open, and a chest. Pay close attention to how the paws are drawn with ovals that look flat.

Step 2

Draw leaf-shaped ears that overlap the corners of the head. Follow by drawing round eyes at the top of the snout. Add a nose and mouth. Draw curved lines on the belly and a curly tail.

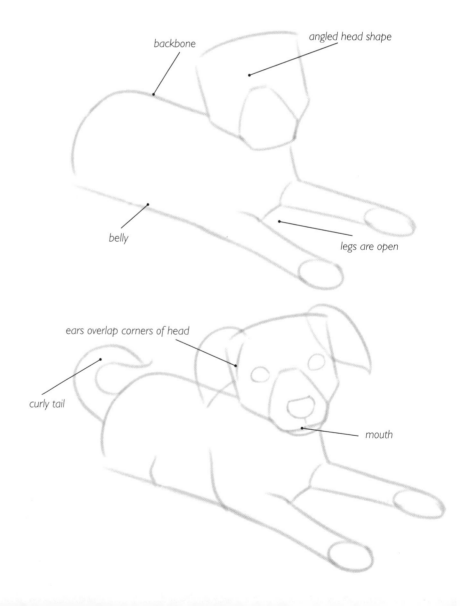

backbone

angled head shape

belly

legs are open

ears overlap corners of head

curly tail

mouth

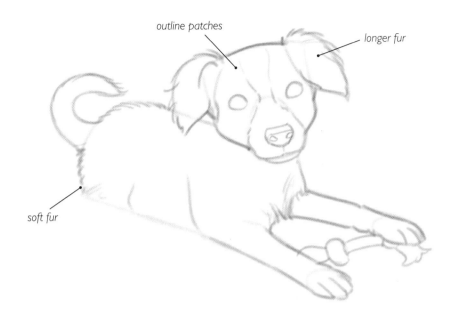

outline patches

longer fur

soft fur

Step 3

Starting at the puppy's bottom, work your way around the outline drawing fur with fine, soft marks. Pay attention to the longer marks on the ears and chest area. Add marks to define patches around the eyes and snout. Draw nostrils, and lines for paws. Underneath the paws, sketch the puppy's toy.

Step 4

Using long, soft pencil lines, draw grass around the belly and legs then draw furry line work in the ears. With light pencil pressure, build up the shadowy gray tone in the grass under the puppy's body. Continue by shading the lighter tone around the edge of the puppy's form. Using medium pencil pressure, shade a medium level of tone for patches over the body. Darken the eyes, nose, and mouth. Once you add the fine, long whiskers and the details for the toy, your puppy will be ready to play!

DRAWING TIP

White highlights make eyes look shiny and round. You create them by leaving areas of the paper clear of pencil shading.

INTERESTING FACT → Irish wolfhounds are considered to be the tallest dog in the world, with the average male standing almost three feet tall!

KITTEN

Kittens make popular family pets because they are lovable and people receive great pleasure from patting the silky fur and hearing a cat's comforting purr. A kitten's playful antics can be adorable to watch as they pounce and romp awkwardly around the place. Their favorite pastimes can be trying to catch an insect or tapping a ball of yarn. When they grow into adults, they can be very handy to have around the place when they start to catch mice!

Before You Begin

The kitten is drawn using a series of solid and rounded shapes. Observe in the first step that the body of the kitten is floating above the baseline to leave room for the legs. Also note that the legs are drawn at two different levels, in front and behind. Getting the positioning of the limbs and face will be very important to achieving the profile of the kitten.

Step 1

Lightly draw a baseline. Draw an oval body on a slight angle above the baseline. Overlap a circle for the head, adding a line for the neck. Sketch a snout from the head to the body. Draw a thick, curved tail shape pointing out from the back.

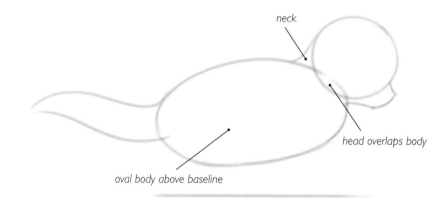

neck

head overlaps body

oval body above baseline

Step 2

Draw an open eye on the head above the snout. Sketch the front pointy ear inside the head and the smaller ear behind on top of the head. Draw the back curved leg with the paw sitting on the baseline. Sketch the front leg and paw raised above the baseline. Add the other legs behind in line with the baseline.

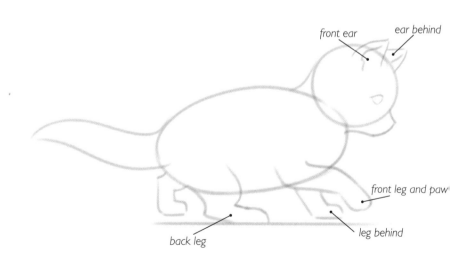

front ear

ear behind

front leg and paw

back leg

leg behind

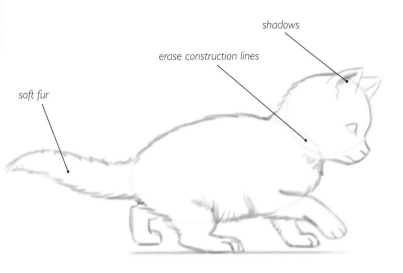

shadows

erase construction lines

soft fur

Step 3

Erase any lines you no longer need. Starting at the tail, use fine, soft furry marks around the kitten's outline. Smooth and define the rest of the kitten's form. Add lines for the nose, mouth, and paws. Draw any other shadows you see.

Step 4

Starting at the tail, use light pencil pressure to shade the soft, furry marks that make the stripy pattern over the kitten's body. Build up a medium level of gray tone under the kitten, on the tail, and around the head. Add details to the eye and draw a collar. Darken the kitten's outline in parts and draw a shadow under its body. Once you draw the fine whiskers and the ball of wool, your kitten will be ready to pounce!

DRAWING TIP

Before you start a drawing, study the different levels of gray tone (light, medium, and dark). Practice sketching the different types of shading on a separate piece of paper.

INTERESTING FACT → Kittens only have sweat glands in the soles of their feet!

More Funky Things to Draw—Cute Critters

TIGER CUB ⭐ ⭐ ⭐

Tigers enjoy living in forest or jungle environments near water and large prey. The black stripes on a tiger's coat camouflage it when it is in the wild. Tigers use their silence and stealth to catch monkeys, birds, reptiles, and fish. Young cubs depend on their mother for the first year of their lives. By the time they are two years old, they have enough strength and power to be able to catch their own prey.

Before You Begin

The tiger cub is constructed using a series of rounded shapes. Study how the shapes overlap the body and the baseline in the second step, and how the tiger's curved outline is contoured around the shapes. Also, pay attention to the oval shapes drawn for paws that are slightly squashed, and how the stripy pattern is evenly spaced across the tiger's form in step 4.

Step 1

With light pencil pressure, draw a baseline. Well above the baseline, sketch a slightly angled and rounded head shape that dips in at the top on both sides. Draw half-circles for ears where the head dips in. From the middle of the head, sketch a snout and mouth shape. Next, add a curved backbone and chest.

Step 2

Closely observe how the legs and paws overlap the body and baseline. Draw a bent hind leg with an oval for the paw. Next to the bent hind leg, draw the leg underneath with a round foot. Draw the front leg shapes on your right, each with an oval paw sitting under the baseline. Sketch a thick tail shape that is bent in the middle, in line with the backbone and trailing back from the hind leg.

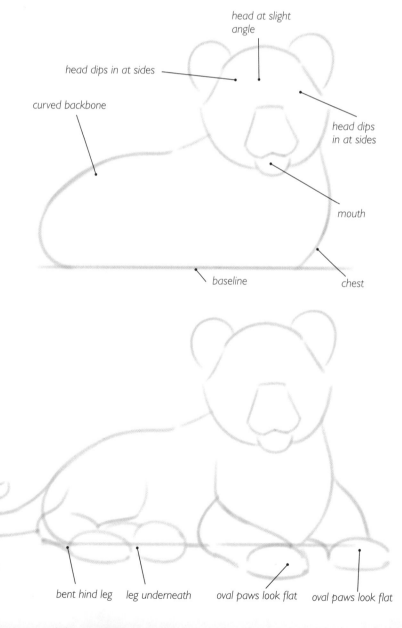

head at slight angle

head dips in at sides

curved backbone

head dips in at sides

mouth

baseline

chest

tail trails back

bent hind leg   leg underneath   oval paws look flat   oval paws look flat

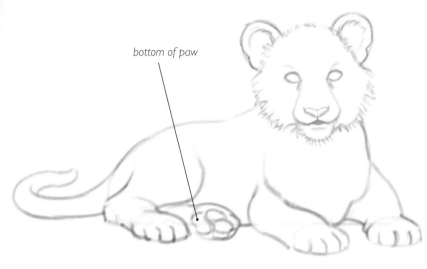

bottom of paw

Step 3

Define and smooth the curved outline of the tiger's form around the shapes. Using fine, soft marks, draw the tiger's furry jowls. Draw almond-shaped eyes at the top of the snout. Add a nose and create an opening for the mouth. Sketch any other fine marks you see. Draw lines inside the ears and add lines to the paws. For the leg underneath, draw the oval shapes for the bottom of the paw.

Step 4

Lightly shade a stripy pattern over the head. Then, starting at the tail, apply the pattern across the body. With medium pencil pressure, shade a medium gray tone inside the ears and around the eyes and snout. Continue by adding shadows under the chin and around the legs and paws. Add dots for eyes and fine whiskers around the snout. Once you draw the jungle in the background, your tiger cub will be ready to hunt for prey!

DRAWING TIP

A pattern is a repeated series of dots, lines, marks, or shapes. It can add detail or areas of interest to a drawing.

INTERESTING FACT → Tigers hunt at night and are able to see much better than people can. Their eyes reflect any light that shines upon them, which makes them glow in the dark.

RABBIT ⭐

A rabbit's physical features are primarily used to sense danger. Their large ears provide excellent hearing. Their eyes are high up on the sides of their head, which allows them almost 360-degree vision, and their long back legs enable them to run at impressive speeds. Even though rabbits are considered to be adorable creatures by most, they have reached pest status in some parts of the world because of their ability to produce up to 30 rabbit kittens in one year.

Before You Begin

The rabbit is constructed using a series of rounded shapes. To achieve the right pose, you must position the facial features and the front legs correctly. Observe how the rabbit sits on the baseline. Notice how the rabbit's body is slightly turned to your left. Also, to make your rabbit look doe-eyed, you must leave areas of white highlights on its pupils.

Step 1

Using light pencil pressure, draw a baseline. A distance above the baseline, sketch a head shape that dips in at the sides. Draw curved lines from under the head to form the body. Closely observe the positioning of the front legs and feet. Draw the front leg shapes in the middle of the body and slightly over to your left. Sketch the feet over the baseline, making sure the one on your right is not touching the outline of the body.

Step 2

Draw floppy ears coming out from the dips in the side of the head. Define and smooth the rabbit's curved outline around the shapes. Notice how the rabbit's bottom pokes out. Form the contoured outline of the hands and feet. Add lines for fingers and toes. Draw a nose and mouth in line with the opening between the hands.

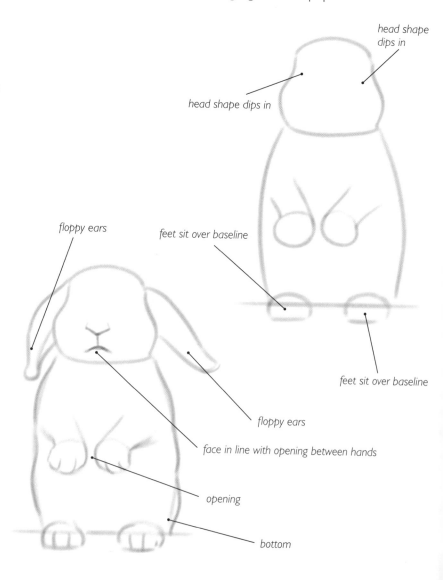

head shape dips in

head shape dips in

floppy ears

feet sit over baseline

feet sit over baseline

floppy ears

face in line with opening between hands

opening

bottom

soft fur

Step 3

Erase any lines you no longer need. Starting at the head, softly draw fine, furry marks around the rabbit's outline. Lightly draw a curved line coming from the mouth and around the nose. Draw ellipses for eyes (flattened ovals) near either side of the head.

Step 4

With medium pencil pressure, shade a dark gray tone inside the eyes, around the nose and mouth, and the side of the head. Make sure you leave white highlights in the pupils. Using light pencil pressure, gently sketch the soft pencil marks for fur around the rabbit's form. Focus on the shadows around the head, face and hands. With a sharp pencil, draw a dot pattern around the mouth and fine long whiskers. Once you draw the field flowers, your rabbit will be ready to run!

DRAWING TIP

To make eyes look shiny and show that there is light reflecting from the pupils, create round white highlights. Draw an outline of the highlight, but leave the paper inside the outline clear and unshaded.

INTERESTING FACT → Rabbits come from an order of animals called lagomorphs. This order also includes hares, pikas, and jackrabbits.

PANDA BEAR

Panda bears live in the remote mountain forests of central China, where there are plenty of bamboo plants for them to munch on. Together, all the pandas in China eat around 22,000 pounds of bamboo every day! Pandas have a thick woolly white and black coat, which allows them to withstand cold and snowy conditions. The panda's coat feels oily and is also waterproof. Sadly, they are endangered because farmers are cutting down the plants they need to survive.

Before You Begin

The panda bear is built using a series of rounded shapes. Study the different types of shapes that are drawn and how they fit together and overlap. Observe how the arms come down from under the jaw and overlap the body. The front leg sits inside the end of the body. Also, pay attention to the angle of the body and where the branches are positioned.

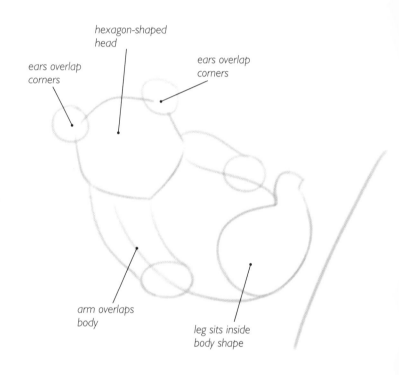

Step 1

Lightly draw a hexagon-shaped head at an angle. Overlap round ears on the corners of the head and connect a jellybean-shaped body at a slight angle. From the head, draw the arm on your left so it overlaps the body. Sketch the arm on your right resting on the belly, making sure the round hand overlaps the belly. Draw a rounded leg shape inside the end of the body with the foot sticking out. Draw the line of the tree trunk at an angle.

Step 2

Define and smooth the curved outline of the panda's form. Pay special attention to the ears and hands. For the hands and foot, add lines to create fingers and toes. Draw round eyes in the middle of the head then draw the nose and mouth underneath. Sketch the curvy lines of the branch behind. Erase any lines you no longer need.

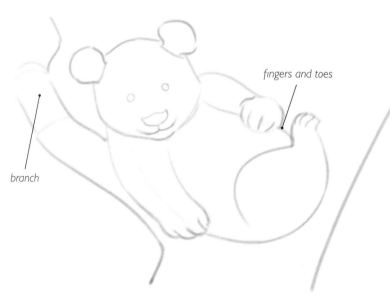

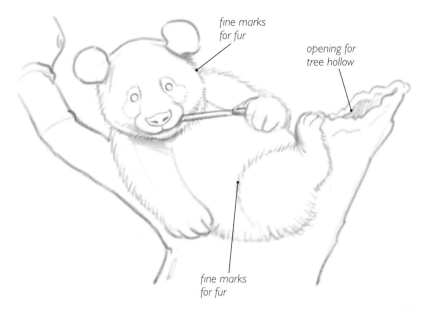

fine marks for fur

opening for tree hollow

fine marks for fur

Step 3

Starting from the head, use light pencil pressure to create soft fine marks for fur. Sketch patches around the eyes and define the snout. Draw nostrils and define the mouth, leaving a small opening for the bamboo. Next, draw the bamboo coming from the mouth and connect it to the hand. Define and smooth the tree trunk, drawing an opening for a hollow.

DRAWING TIP

Some drawings may seem difficult because of the detail. With practice, your skills will improve and you will feel more confident when tackling detailed drawings.

Step 4

Study the level of medium gray tone covering the panda's body. With medium pencil pressure, shade the patches on the panda's body from head to toe. Darken the eyes, mouth, and areas around the hands and foot. Darken and define the outline of the fur. Using light pencil pressure, shade lighter gray tones around the head and belly and under the bamboo. Once you shade a light wood texture on the trunk and the mountains in the background, your panda will be ready to munch bamboo!

INTERESTING FACT → Panda bears have five fingers and two thumbs on each hand! The second thumb is a growth that comes out of the wrist, which allows them to grab onto bamboo stems as they strip off the leaves.

More Funky Things to Draw—Cute Critters

LAMB ⭐⭐

Lambs are born during springtime and are usually twins. Within a few minutes of being born, they are ready to stand up. The mother licks her babies clean and then helps them to their feet by gently nudging them with her nose. For around four months, lambs drink their mother's milk until they are old enough to eat tender grass. Lambs enjoy frolicking in the pasture with their friends and will bleat loudly so the mother ewe can hear when they are in trouble.

Before You Begin

Be careful to draw the first step correctly, as it will help you achieve the right perspective. Study step 1 carefully. You will see that the back legs are thinner and shorter than the front legs. You must draw the front legs first so they guide you in positioning the back legs. Also, pay special attention to the different types of soft, furry marks that are drawn for the wool in step 4.

Step 1

Lightly draw the head shape. Draw the chest arching out from the head, making sure it is straight on the bottom. Lightly sketch a baseline a distance under the chest. Draw the thick front legs down to the baseline. Draw a second baseline parallel with the front baseline. Position one back leg between the front legs. Next, draw a curved shape for the other back leg on an angle, coming down from the top of the chest.

Step 2

Define and smooth the lamb's curvy outline around the shapes. Add details for the toes and the wavy lines inside the ears. Don't forget the fold in the belly area. Erase any unwanted line work.

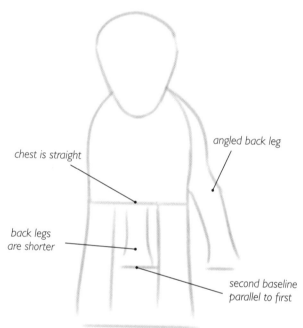

chest is straight

angled back leg

back legs are shorter

second baseline parallel to first

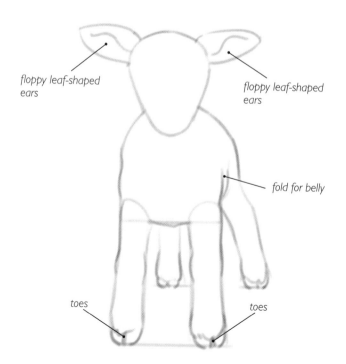

floppy leaf-shaped ears

floppy leaf-shaped ears

fold for belly

toes

toes

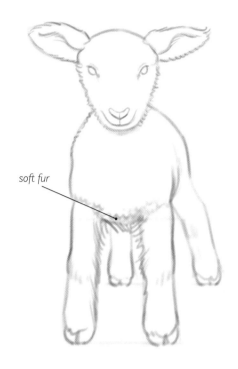

soft fur

Step 3

Observe the soft, furry outline that has been drawn around the chest, front legs, head, and ears. Using light pencil pressure, start at the ears and work your way down by adding the fine marks that create the texture of the wool. Draw the almond shaped-eyes on either side of the head. Next, draw the nose and mouth.

DRAWING TIP

Before you begin applying texture or shading for fur or hair, practice the different types of marks you see on your subject on a separate piece of paper.

Step 4

Pay special attention to the different marks and shading that have been applied to the lamb's form. Define and darken the eyes and nose area. With light pencil pressure, work your way down from the head, applying light gray tone and soft, furry marks. Using a medium pencil grip, shade a medium gray tone inside the ears, around the chin and belly, and under the chest. Once you add the lamb's shadow and the field, your lamb will be ready to frolic!

INTERESTING FACT ⟶ Lambs are born with eight milk teeth that are similar to human baby teeth.

More Funky Things to Draw—Cute Critters

KOALA ⭐⭐

Koalas are Australian mammals that live in eucalyptus trees. Koalas are often called "koala bears," but this is incorrect. In fact they are marsupials, which means that like kangaroos, their young are born very small and grow inside a pouch on their mother's belly. Koala fur is thick and soft to touch and they have sharp claws on their fingers to help them grip and move up trees. Koalas spend most of their day asleep and move around after sunset.

Before You Begin

The most important aspect of this drawing is the way that the koala's form is anchored to the tree branch. The koala's body sits against the branch and its limbs are connected to it. Observe the width of the solid, round body and the distance between the head and the branch. Also, pay attention to how the arm wraps around the tree and how the foot is connected.

Step 1

Lightly draw curved lines for the branch. Draw a geometric head shape on a slight angle, joining half-circles for ears. Sketch a line across the face and draw a rounded backbone from the ear around to the branch. Sketch the shoulder on your left against the tree, with the hand wrapping around the branch. Add a round belly. Draw a rounded arm near the backbone. Next, sketch the curved outline of the leg, with the foot overlapping the branch.

Step 2

Draw the fingers and toes inside the shapes for the hands and foot. Starting at the head, work around the outline to define and smooth the koala's form. Continue by creating the bumps in the line work of the branch. Over the line on the face, draw almond-shaped eyes at a slight angle. Draw the nose shape followed by a smiling mouth. Don't forget the line work inside the ears.

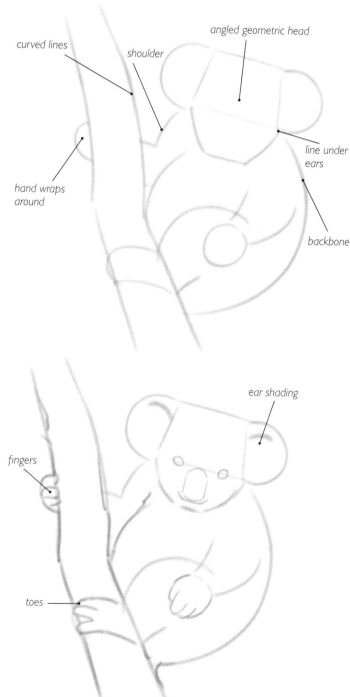

curved lines

shoulder

angled geometric head

line under ears

hand wraps around

backbone

ear shading

fingers

toes

fine fur

Step 3

With a clean eraser, remove any line work you no longer need. Starting at the head, begin drawing fine furry marks around the koala's outline. Define the sides of the head and the nose and mouth area.

DRAWING TIP

Remember not to press too hard on your pencil when beginning a drawing, as it will make it difficult to erase any mistakes.

Step 4

Study the soft marks that create the texture of the koala's fur. Notice how they are darker on the koala's bottom and ears. Starting at the head, use light pencil pressure to make the light gray marks for fur around the body. Use a medium pencil grip to draw the darker areas around the body. Darken the eyes and nose then add sharp claws wrapping around the branch, and sketch in the second branch. Once you add texture for the bark and leaves, your koala will be ready to climb!

INTERESTING FACT → Koalas spend most of the day resting because the two pounds of eucalyptus leaves they eat each day don't give them much energy.

RED FOX CUB

Baby fox cubs (also called kits or pups) are born blind and rely entirely on their mother for food because they don't open their eyes to the world until they're two weeks old. The mother fox, called a vixen, gives birth to around 13 cubs at one time. At three weeks of age, fox cubs begin establishing an order of dominance by viciously fighting with each other. They are ready to leave the den at four weeks, venturing outside to pounce on insects and carry around sticks and leaves.

Before You Begin

The form of the fox is built using a series of solid shapes. The two most important aspects of this drawing are the angle of the head and the way the body sits on the baseline. This will help you to create the correct perspective. Also, pay special attention to how the curves of the fox's body are contoured around the solid shapes.

Step 1

Using light pencil pressure, draw a baseline. Sketch a geometric shaped head on an angle above the baseline. Notice that the jaw is v-shaped. Lightly draw a "T" in the middle of the facial area and add pointy ears. Draw a curved outline for the body shape, sitting it on the baseline. Sketch the curved leg shapes inside the body with the paws sitting below the baseline.

Step 2

Draw a back paw on the baseline, positioning it behind the front left leg (on your right). Sketch the round eyes either side of the "T" and a snout sitting inside the "V" shaped jaw. Add a nose, and curved lines inside the ears. Draw a curved tail coming from behind the body, touching the back paw.

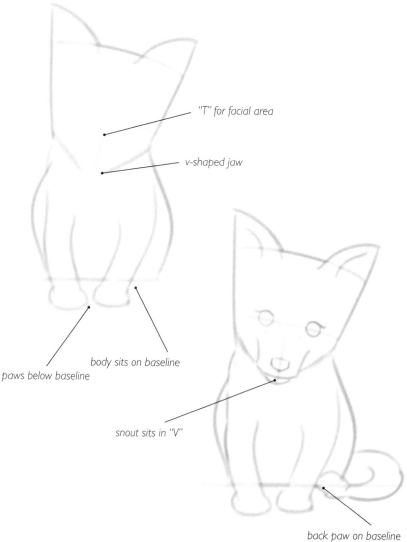

"T" for facial area

v-shaped jaw

body sits on baseline

paws below baseline

snout sits in "V"

back paw on baseline

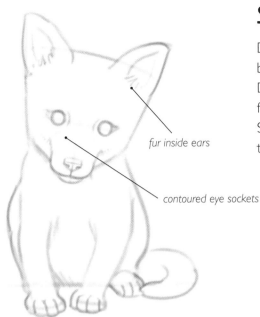

fur inside ears

contoured eye sockets

Step 3

Define and smooth the curves of the fox's outline around the body. Pay attention to the contours of the ears, legs, and paws. Define the details of the nose and snout. Lightly sketch fine marks for fur inside the ears and softly shape the contoured eye sockets. Sketch soft marks around the chest and draw lines for toes inside the paws.

DRAWING TIP

Texture refers to the look and feel of a surface. The types of marks you make, like fine lines or gentle shading, create the texture of soft fur.

Step 4

Study the various levels of shading over the fox's body, observing how some areas are left white. Create the fine marks for fur around the outline. Darken and define the pupils, nose, and snout. Continue by gently building up the medium level of shading inside the ears, on the paws, and under the body. With lighter pencil pressure, create the softer levels of shading from head to toe. Add fine lines for whiskers. Draw the tree trunk in the front of the picture (the foreground). Once you add the wavy grass and the leaves in the background, your fox cub will be ready to pounce!

INTERESTING FACT → The vixen prepares a few dens before the cubs are born, eventually choosing the one with the best water drainage.

More Funky Things to Draw—Cute Critters

MOUSE ⭐

Mice belong to a group of animal called rodents. Other animals in this group are squirrels, guinea pigs, and beavers. Mice have a long history of being written about in children's stories as cute little characters, but in real life they can be destructive pests that damage crops. They mainly feed on plant life but are also happy to eat dairy, meat, and fruit. Mice are amazing climbers, jumpers, and swimmers, and use their long tail to help them balance.

Before You Begin

The mouse is constructed using a series of rounded shapes. It is important to carefully observe these shapes before you start to draw, so you achieve the correct perspective. Also, study how the mouse is perched on the corner of the bench and the positions of its limbs.

Step 1

Lightly draw the sharp corner of the bench top. Draw a rounded shape for the head, making sure it is flat on top. Sketch an angled line for the front of the body and a curved line for the back that drops over the edge of the bench. On the top of the head, draw a flattened ellipse for the ear on your left and a larger oval for the one on your right. Add lines for the backs of the ears.

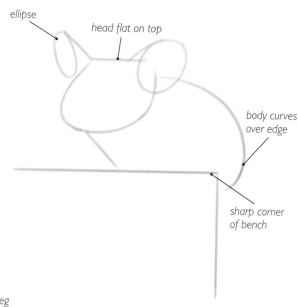

ellipse

head flat on top

body curves over edge

sharp corner of bench

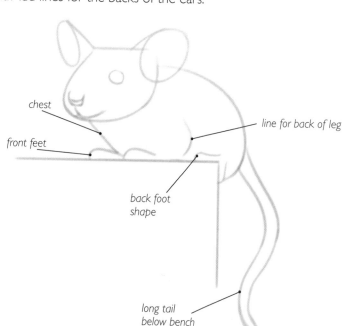

chest

front feet

line for back of leg

back foot shape

long tail below bench

Step 2

Draw a round eye near the top of the head. Sketch curved lines for the nose at the front of the head, and the mouth below them. Draw a bump for the foot in front of the chest. Add a second foot next to the first. Sketch a line for the back of the leg and the back foot shape sitting on the corner of the bench. Draw a long wavy tail shape hanging below the bench.

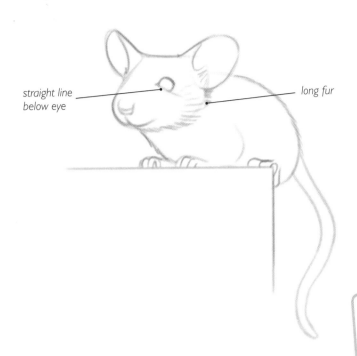

straight line below eye — long fur

Step 3

Define and darken the outline of the mouse around the shapes. Sketch long hairy marks for fur around the ears, face and body. Draw a straight line across the bottom of the eye and define the top of the eye. Draw lines for toes inside the feet.

DRAWING TIP

Don't allow your pencil to get too blunt during the drawing process. Sharpen pencils when the lead starts to become flattened on the end.

Step 4

With medium pencil pressure, darken the eye, nose, and mouth. Continue by shading a medium gray tone inside the ear and under the chin and body. Using a light pencil grip, softly draw the fine, long marks for fur from head to toe. Next, lightly add any further shading around the body that you can see. Once you add whisker marks and a wood pattern on the bench, your mouse will be ready to search for food!

INTERESTING FACT → Mice don't like bright lights and have little or no color vision because they are mainly nocturnal animals.

RACCOON ★ ★ ★

Raccoons are often called "bandits" because of their boldly masked faces. This is a perfect title for them as they are skillful in breaking into people's homes and farmers' food stores to steal food. Raccoons live close to water and use their nimble fingers to catch fish, insects, and frogs. As they will eat almost anything, a common place to find them is at the local dump. Raccoons often make their homes in tree hollows where they give birth to their young.

Before You Begin

Observe the rounded shapes of the raccoon's form and how it hangs over the tree branch. It is important that you draw the tree and branch first and then sit the raccoon's body in the fork of the tree. Notice also how the tail that hangs under the branch is in line with the backbone. Closely study the various fine marks that are applied for fur in the final step.

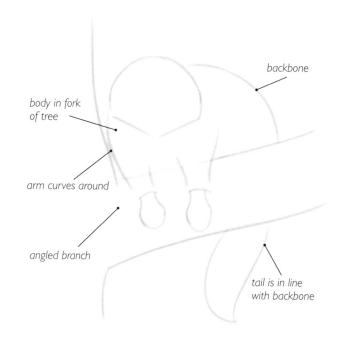

backbone

body in fork
of tree

arm curves around

angled branch

tail is in line
with backbone

Step 1

Lightly draw the outline of the tree trunk, with a branch at an angle. Draw a round head shape with a pointy jaw above the fork in the tree. From the top of the head, draw a curved backbone around to the branch. Sketch the tail under the branch in line with the backbone. Sketch the shapes for arms, hanging over the branch. Notice how the arm on your left curves around from the backbone.

Step 2

Sketch a squarish looking nose in the point of the jaw. Follow by drawing round eyes in the middle of the head with a furry outline around them. Draw pointy ears with a line around the inside. Lightly draw fine, furry marks for jowls and inside the ears. Draw five sharp claws inside both hand shapes.

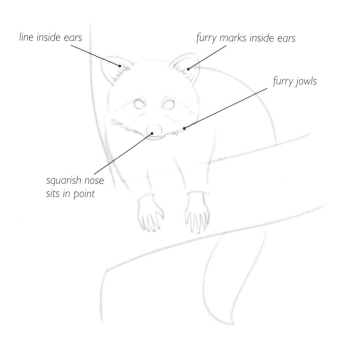

line inside ears

furry marks inside ears

furry jowls

squarish nose
sits in point

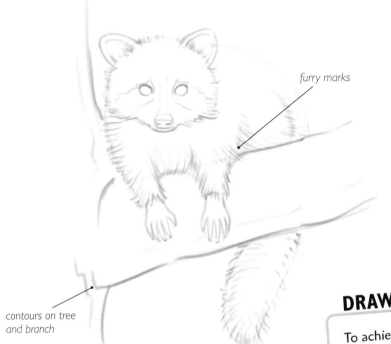

furry marks

contours on tree and branch

Step 3

Starting at the head and working your way down the body, lightly draw fine furry marks around the raccoon's outline. Observe how some furry marks are applied inside the chest area and on the belly and tail. Further define the shape of the nose and nostrils. Define and smooth the contours of the tree trunk and branch.

DRAWING TIP

To achieve fine, sharp lines for whiskers and fur, use a freshly sharpened pencil. A blunter pencil is better for shading smooth levels of gray tone.

Step 4

Observe the different levels of gray tone applied over the raccoon's form. Starting at the head, lightly draw the fine marks over the face, leaving white areas clear. Continue by making fine marks over the body then build up medium levels of tone under the chin and around the raccoon's outline. With a medium pencil grip, shade a medium tone for the mask, ears, tail, and fingers. Add dark tone to the eyes and nose, and fine lines for whiskers. Once you add texture for bark, your raccoon will be ready to forage!

INTERESTING FACT → Raccoons have a habit of examining their food before they eat it, and dipping it in water to wash it.

More Funky Things to Draw

Wedding Day

Paul Könye • Kate Ashforth

More Funky Things to Draw

Wedding Day

More Funky Things to Draw—Wedding Day

INTRODUCTION

Many people love to daydream about weddings: the clothes, the wedding party, the cake. Dream weddings of glamour and extravagance have significantly evolved in the last century. When Queen Victoria of England was married in 1840, she started many new trends, such as the tiered wedding cake, the bride's white lace dress, and the flower girl dressing just like the bride. Weddings are often grand affairs that are planned months in advance, with couples putting their own signature touches on their special day.

THINGS YOU WILL NEED

- A gray lead pencil (HB or 2B).
- A pencil sharpener and a dish for shavings.
- Sheets of drawing paper.
- A clean eraser.
- Patience—learning drawing skills takes time and practice.
- Confidence—a positive attitude will help to develop your drawing skills!

Drawing Guidelines

1 There is a process in learning to draw. Follow the steps carefully and in order.
2 Always use light pencil pressure when beginning the first stage of a drawing.
3 If you feel unsure about the instructions, ask an adult for help.
4 Gray lead smudges easily. Pay attention to where your hand is on the page.
5 Clean the gray lead residue off your eraser by rubbing it against a spare piece of paper.
6 Most of the directions for drawing people don't mention the joints of the limbs or the hand and feet shapes, but they're still important! Be sure to draw them in.

 Beginner   Intermediate Expert

The stars at the top of each page grade the difficulty level of each drawing from beginner to intermediate or expert. Some drawings are trickier than others because of the level of detail, but if you carefully follow the basic principles of building a drawing from shapes and lines, you will learn to conquer both simple and complex drawings.

Follow the Steps

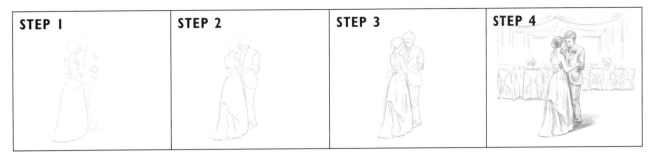

Throughout the following pages, you will find a variety of human subjects as well as objects such as a wedding cake. To draw the human form, you need to construct a "skeleton" using a series of joints, lines, and shapes. For subjects that have a structural framework, study the sizes and types of shapes that are drawn. You must position all parts of a drawing correctly to create its whole form.

PENCIL TECHNIQUES FOR DRAWING PEOPLE AND STRUCTURES

The boxes below show three types of shapes drawn for inanimate objects.

| layered ellipses | irregular shapes | boxy shapes |

When you arrive at each page of this book, observe the types of shapes drawn for each subject. Study how they connect or are layered. Also, look at the lengths, widths, and directions of all the lines and shapes.

A wide variety of shapes are drawn for different subjects. Ellipses (flattened ovals) are drawn for parts of the human form or for the structure of a cake. Irregular shapes are used to draw organic elements like leaves or flowers.

Shading and Pencil Pressure

Shading adds detail and definition to a subject. Apply different levels of shading with changes in pencil pressure—a light pencil grip creates a light gray tone, for example.

The boxes below show different levels of grey tone created by a change in pencil pressure.

Light   Medium   Dark

More Funky Things to Draw—Wedding Day

THE BRIDE ⭐⭐

In ancient times, marriages were bartered for like a piece of land, and a man would pay a woman's father for her hand in marriage. Marriages are now far more eventful and extravagant affairs that celebrate romance. Many girls grow up looking forward to the day they will meet their perfect match and get married. Becoming a bride allows a woman to feel and act like a princess for a day, carrying flowers and wearing jewels and a beautiful gown.

Before You Begin

The most important aspects of drawing the bride are the positioning of the spine and face and the angle of the shoulders and hips. These will help you correctly draw the bride's pose. Also, to make the bride's train look like it is sitting flat against the floor, you must position it properly over the bottom of the wedding dress.

Step 1

Lightly draw a circle for the bride's head. Sketch a pointed chin that faces to your right. Draw a cross for the face and a spine curving down from behind the chin. Draw shoulders at an angle and add the upper arms and elbows. Sketch hips parallel to the shoulders with a cone-shaped skirt below. Lightly draw an ellipse over the bottom of the skirt and out to your left. Finish the bride's right arm.

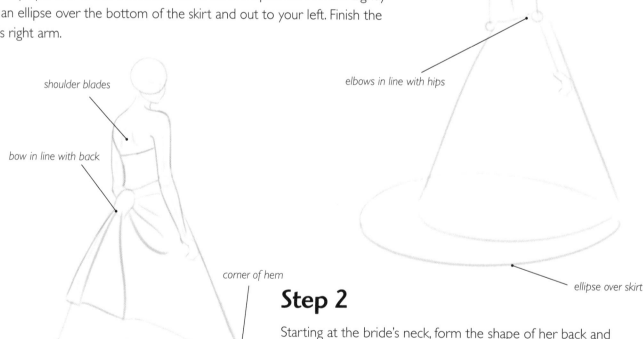

spine behind chin

elbows in line with hips

ellipse over skirt

shoulder blades

bow in line with back

corner of hem

Step 2

Starting at the bride's neck, form the shape of her back and arms over the skeleton. Erase the spine, then re-draw it lightly with shoulder blades on either side. Draw a line for the top of the dress and sketch the bow in line with her back. Draw a curved line from the bow to the corner of the hemline.

facial features over cross

bodice

folds of train

scalloped hem

Step 3

Draw eyes on either side of the facial cross, followed by the nose and mouth. Define the outline of the bride's face and draw wavy hair around her head and neck. Sketch a tiara curving over her head. Draw fingers inside the hand shape and a bouquet hanging down. Add detail to the bodice and bow. Sketch a scalloped hemline around the bottom of the ellipse. Softly shade the folds of the train.

DRAWING TIP

As you go, remember to erase any lines that you no longer need so they don't interfere with your final drawing.

Step 4

Define the details of the bride's facial features. Draw a dark wavy line pattern for the bride's hair and define her bouquet. Use light pencil pressure to shade the highlights of her skin and the folds and creases of her dress. Pay attention to the pattern around the corset and scalloped hemline. Next, draw the lines of the floorboards. Once you add the shadow and the rest of the background, your bride will be ready to get married!

INTERESTING FACT → It is still considered to be bad luck for a man to see his fiancée in her bridal gown prior to the ceremony.

More Funky Things to Draw—Wedding Day

THE GROOM

In the past it was traditional for a man to ask a woman's father for her hand in marriage. Now both men and women can ask directly: "Will you marry me?" The most common outfit for a groom is a well-tailored, dark-colored suit. Flowers for the buttonhole and the color of the tie are often chosen to complement the bride's gown. At an evening wedding, a groom may wear a tuxedo with a bow tie and cummerbund.

Before You Begin

The drawing of the groom is based around a spine and a series of chunky shapes. You will observe that his body is turned slightly to the side but his head is facing you. One arm is slightly hidden and the other is in full view.

Step 1

Lightly draw a circle for the groom's head. Draw a chin shape at a slight angle and draw a facial cross at the same angle. Next, sketch a spine curving down, with guidelines for shoulders and hips. Draw the shape of the torso over the spine. Add the hidden arm and then the one in front. Draw the legs and hand shape.

Step 2

Define and darken the outline of the groom's suit around the shapes. Starting at the head, define the neck and create the collar. Draw lapels over the front of the torso and draw the front hem of the jacket below the hand. Add a zigzag for the vest.

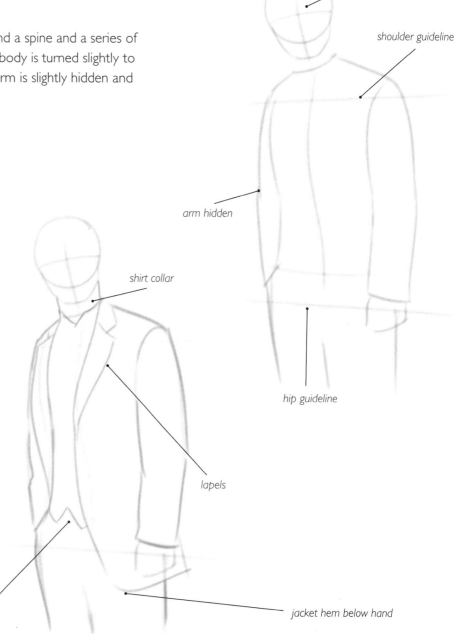

facial cross

shoulder guideline

arm hidden

shirt collar

hip guideline

lapels

vest

jacket hem below hand

hair curves around forehead

folds in suit

folds in suit

fingers inside hand shape

Step 3

Define the shape of the groom's head and the curves of his hair around the forehead. Add ears and draw eyes on either side of the cross. Follow with the nose and mouth. Create the vest and add a tie at the top. Draw a pocket handkerchief and the fingers inside the hand shape. Sketch the creases and folds in the suit.

DRAWING TIP

When you draw a cross on a face, it acts as a guideline for the facial features.

Step 4

Using light pencil pressure, shade the texture of the groom's hair and define his facial features. Starting at the head, lightly shade the highlights and shadows of his skin and clothing. Concentrate on the folds in his suit. Draw a boutonniere (buttonhole flower), and buttons on the vest. Lightly draw a brick wall in the background, and if you feel like challenging yourself, sketch the three groomsmen. Your groom is now ready for his big day!

INTERESTING FACT → The tradition of going down on one knee before proposing goes back to the custom of kneeling before royalty.

FLOWER GIRL

At many weddings, a young girl walks ahead of the wedding party scattering flower petals for the bride and groom to walk on. The flower girl often wears or carries a floral hoop, which symbolizes a wedding ring and eternal love. She usually wears a white dress as a symbol of youth and innocence, and her flowers give the ceremony an extra touch of beauty and fragrance. This is a lovely way to let younger relatives participate in the wedding ceremony.

Before You Begin

The flower girl is built around a skeleton and a dress shape. She looks like she is walking. To achieve this, you need to draw the spine at a slight angle and draw her arms, legs, hands, and feet correctly.

Step 1

Lightly draw a circle for the flower girl's head with a chin shape below. Draw a facial cross looking to your right. Draw a spine curving down with shoulders at a slight angle. Draw the dress shape and sketch the arms, paying attention to their length and angle. The arm on your right is foreshortened. Draw the legs with the foot on your left slightly forward and the other one behind.

Step 2

Define the outline of the flower girl's dress, adding a fold in the skirt, a wavy hemline, and puffed shoulders. Don't forget the waistband. Form her neck, arms, and legs around the skeleton. Under her forearm, sketch an ellipse for the basket that overlaps her dress. Draw a handle for the basket curving through her hand.

angled spine

foreshortened arm

open hand

foot in front

handle curves through hand

ellipse for basket

garland

facial features over cross

fingers curl around handle

waistband

Step 3

Draw eyes on either side of the cross, followed by a nose and open mouth. Draw the flower garland over the top of the flower girl's head and softly draw the outline of the hair below. Define the waistband and lightly shade the folds of her dress. Draw fingers curling around the handle and create the details of the basket. Define the open hand and sketch the shoes.

DRAWING TIP

Foreshortening means that you draw something smaller if you're looking at it head-on. This gives the suggestion that the part nearer to you is hiding the parts further away.

Step 4

Draw eyes looking to your right and gently define the facial features. Darken the garland and shade a line pattern for hair texture. With light pencil pressure, shade tone across the basket and darken her shoes. Softly draw a flagstone floor pattern that gets smaller in the background. Create shadows under her chin, on her legs, and under her figure. Once you add petals and the bush in the background, your flower girl will be ready to scatter her blossoms!

INTERESTING FACT → The flower girl often wears a miniature version of the bride's wedding gown.

More Funky Things to Draw—Wedding Day

WALKING DOWN THE AISLE

Brides are often escorted by their fathers, recalling the old days when marriages were a contract arranged by the bride's family. The groom stands at the top of the aisle waiting anxiously for the beautiful bride to appear. As the wedding procession begins, the friends and family turn around to see the flower girl, the bridesmaids and groomsmen, the maid of honor and the best man, and finally the bride and her father.

Before You Begin

The drawing of the father and the bride is a complex one because of the perspective. It is important that you study the profiles and front and back viewpoints of all the people, and the types of shapes that are used to draw them. Carefully observe how the aisle gets narrower and the pews become smaller toward the back of the drawing. One of the father's legs is shorter to show that he is taking a step.

Step 1

Lightly draw two circles for heads with the bride's a little lower. Add their necks, shoulder lines, and hip lines, paying attention to the different angles. Draw the bride's dress shape and train. Sketch the father's jacket and arms and draw the bride's arms. Sketch the father's legs, paying attention to their length and the backs of the knees. Draw the end of the aisle and then sketch the sides of the pews.

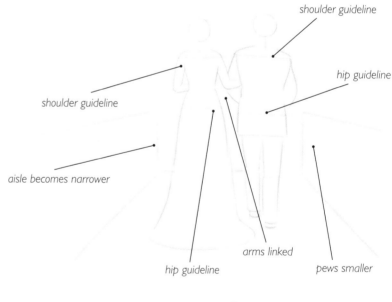

shoulder guideline

hip guideline

shoulder guideline

aisle becomes narrower

arms linked

hip guideline

pews smaller

Step 2

Draw the slight profile of the father followed by his hair, ears, and neck. Define the outline of his suit, paying attention to the creases and bumps in the fabric. Draw the wavy shape of the bride's hair and define her curved outline. Don't forget her shoulder blades and the scalloped hem of her train.

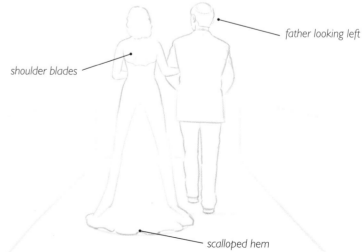

father looking left

shoulder blades

scalloped hem

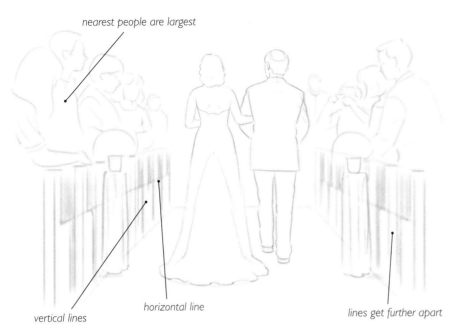

nearest people are largest

vertical lines

horizontal line

lines get further apart

Step 3

Begin drawing at the far end of the aisle. Lightly draw the horizontal line that runs along the middle of the pews. Draw the vertical lines, making sure they get wider as you go. Sketch the pillars with a half-circle shape on top. Softly add shading. Draw the outline of all the guests, layering their bodies as you go. Notice that the nearest people are the largest.

Step 4

With light pencil pressure, build up the medium gray tone over areas of the father's suit and the bride's hair. Add the lacy details around the dress and sketch the soft folds and line around the train. Softly draw the central arched window followed by the smaller ones on either side. Define the pillars and draw the flowers inside the half-circle. Softly add the details to the guests' figures. Once you add the groom and shade the edges, your bride will be ready to walk to the altar!

DRAWING TIP

In drawing, perspective refers to making a flat image look as though it has depth. For example, a pathway seems to narrow as it goes into the distance.

INTERESTING FACT → Many wedding traditions are modified to suit modern tastes. It is not unusual these days for both parents to walk their daughter down the aisle.

WEDDING RINGS

Wedding rings are a symbol of eternity, as they have no beginning and no end. The custom of the wedding ring appears in many different cultures. In India, brides often wear toe rings! Originally only women wore wedding rings, but now it's very common for men to wear them as well. Once a couple agree to marry, they may wear engagement rings and add a wedding band on the day of the marriage ceremony.

Before You Begin

The most important aspects of this drawing are the angle of the cushion and the shading that makes it look three-dimensional. Carefully observe the outline of the cushion and the lines that curve over the middle and around the edges.

Step 1

Lightly draw four slightly curved lines that meet in pinched corners. Observe that the cushion looks slightly flattened. Draw a curved line over the bottom of the cushion.

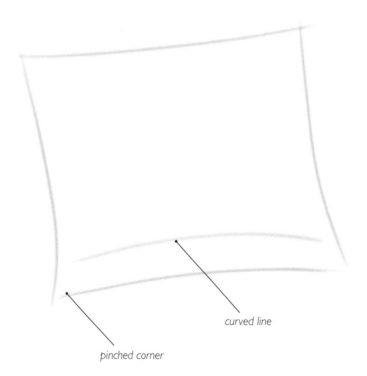

curved line

pinched corner

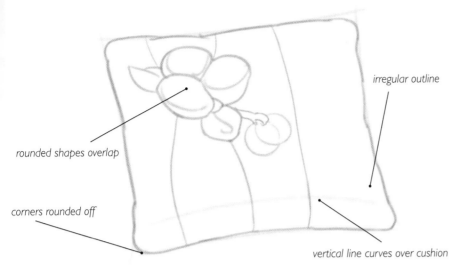

rounded shapes overlap

corners rounded off

irregular outline

vertical line curves over cushion

Step 2

Define the irregular outline of the cushion, making sure the corners are rounded. Draw the three overlapping rounded shapes in the top left corner. Add the leaf shapes on either side. Sketch the loop with two round ring shapes that overlap. Draw three curved lines over the cushion.

Step 3

To create the roses, draw lines spiraling inside the rounded shapes. Define the leaves, loop, and rings. With light pencil pressure, shade small impressions around the edges of the cushion. Build up the large highlight that runs across the base of the cushion and shade gray tone over and around the flowers, leaves, and rings.

DRAWING TIP

Look through magazines and on the internet for ideas about different wedding rings. Not all wedding rings are gold bands!

INTERESTING FACT → The Romans believed that the vein from the fourth finger traveled to the heart, so this is the finger that wedding rings are usually worn on.

BRIDESMAIDS

In ancient Rome, friends of the bride and groom would attend the wedding wearing similar clothes to confuse evil spirits. The role of bridesmaids in modern times is very different. The bride's sisters or dearest friends are often asked to be bridesmaids and given special duties. Sometimes the bride gives them gifts to thank them for their efforts. Bridesmaids wear dresses that complement the bride's gown and are usually brightly colored. They also carry their own bouquets.

Before You Begin

The drawing of the bridesmaids is complex. The three figures are connected and all are positioned differently. Each one is built around a skeleton and a large skirt shape. Carefully observe the angles of all of their heads, shoulders, and arms. Notice also that the knee areas of the seated bridesmaids are bent over the edge of the seat, and that there are many folds in all of their clothing.

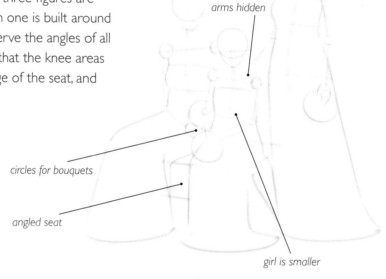

arms hidden

circles for bouquets

angled seat

girl is smaller

Step 1

Lightly draw three parallel angled lines for the seat. Draw a circle and chin for the middle girl's head and a cross for her face. Then draw a spine down to the seat. Draw angled shoulders, a waistline, and arms holding a circle for the bouquet. Next, add her skirt shape with a curved hem. Draw the other seated bridesmaid, who is taller, and then the bridesmaid who is standing and turned slightly away. Note that their arms are hidden behind the seated girl.

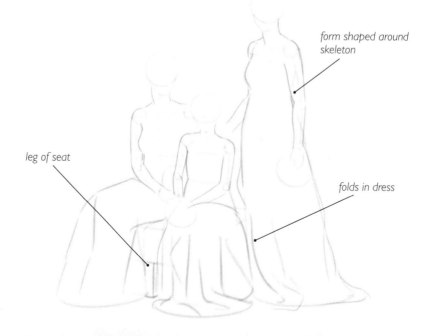

form shaped around skeleton

leg of seat

folds in dress

Step 2

Shape the forms of the bridesmaids' bodies around the skeletons. For each one, start at the neck and work your way down to the hem, creating the curves of their bodies and folds of their dresses as you go. Don't forget the leg of the seat.

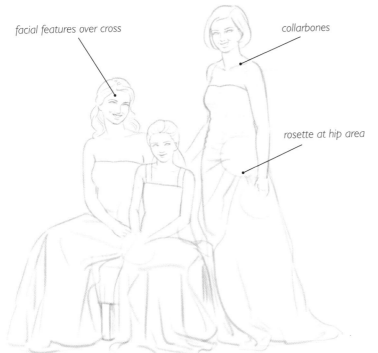

facial features over cross

collarbones

rosette at hip area

Step 3

Draw facial features over each bridesmaid's facial cross. Start with the brow and then add the eyes, nose, and mouth. Sketch their collarbones and add fingers to their hands. Draw their wavy hair around the head circles. Draw rosettes on their hips and add further folds to all their dresses.

DRAWING TIP

When you encounter a picture that is difficult to draw, study each stage of the drawing before you begin, and look at what changes from one step to the next.

Step 4

Define their facial features, adding shading as you go. With light pencil pressure, shade light to medium highlights to create hair texture. Softly shade shadows over their skin. Shade a light horizontal line pattern across the bodices of their dresses. Draw roses inside the bouquets, adding shading as you go. Add detail to their rosettes and add soft light gray tone down the folds of their dresses. Once you shade the seat and a shadow beneath them, your bridesmaids will be ready to pose!

INTERESTING FACT → The maid of honor (or matron of honor, if she is married) is like a chief bridesmaid who helps with important wedding preparations. She may also witness the signing of the marriage license or contract.

WEDDING BOUQUET

The wedding bouquet is an important part of completing a bride's image. Flowers are chosen for their shape, color, and scent. Some of the most traditional wedding flowers are roses, lilies, tulips, and peonies. Flowers are arranged with other foliage and are cut neatly and bound tightly with ribbon. A variety of styles are used for wedding bouquets, but most brides choose traditional and simple designs that complement their wedding gowns.

Before You Begin

The wedding bouquet is structured around a circle and the figure of the bride is hidden behind it. When you start drawing the flowers, begin in the middle and work your way out. Also, draw all the details inside and around the flowers before shading in the gray tone.

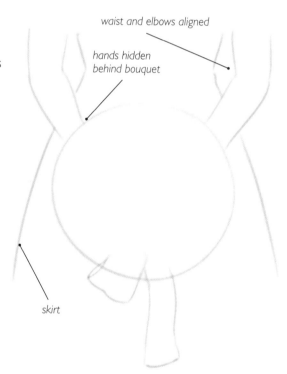

waist and elbows aligned

hands hidden behind bouquet

skirt

Step 1

Lightly draw a circle with ribbon hanging below. At the top, sketch bent shapes for arms on either side of the circle. Draw bent lines for the waist in line with the elbows. Draw lines on either side of the circle for the skirt.

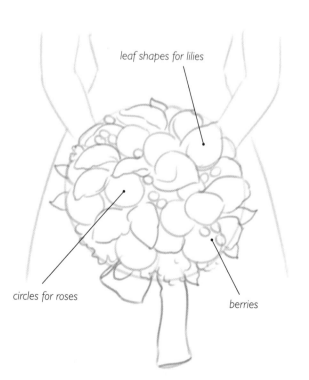

leaf shapes for lilies

circles for roses

berries

Step 2

Begin drawing the leaf shapes and circles, fanning them out to the edge of the circle as you go. Notice that some overlap. Add small circles for berries and leaves in between the flowers and around the edge.

Step 3

Draw spirals inside the circles to create the roses. Define the outline of the roses and add detail to the berries and leaves. Add stamens inside the lilies. With light pencil pressure, build up the light to medium gray tone inside and around the flowers.

DRAWING TIP

Try adding different flower varieties to the bouquet or creating new bouquet designs. Often the bride carries a different bouquet to her bridesmaids!

INTERESTING FACT → It's common for the bride to throw her wedding bouquet over her shoulder at the end of the reception. The belief is that the woman who catches it will get married soon.

More Funky Things to Draw—Wedding Day

WEDDING CAKE

In medieval England, wedding guests would pile up small cakes or sweet rolls, and the bride and groom would try to kiss over the pile without knocking it down. This became the multi-layered wedding cake of today. Such a cake makes a grand statement with its thick white icing, tiers, and decorative flowers and ribbons. The bride and groom cut the cake together to symbolize their new partnership.

Before You Begin

The wedding cake is seen from above, as though you're looking down at the table. The ellipses and construction lines help to build its form and must be drawn correctly. Observe the different sizes of the ellipses and the oval outline of the cake base. Note that the ellipses are flatter at the top to give the cake its perspective.

Step 1

Lightly draw a vertical construction line. From the top, draw five horizontal construction lines. Draw the bottom oval for the cake stand. Next, draw the outline of the plate and the ellipse inside. Follow with the three ellipses for the tiers, making them smaller and flatter as they get to the top.

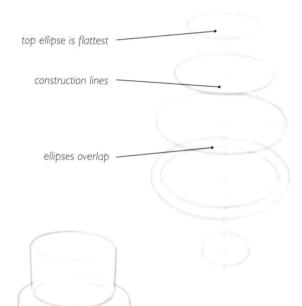

top ellipse is flattest

construction lines

ellipses overlap

Step 2

Draw a curve around the edge of the cake plate and add the pillar underneath. Starting with the largest tier, sketch vertical lines for the sides of each tier and add the curved outlines of the upper and lower edges.

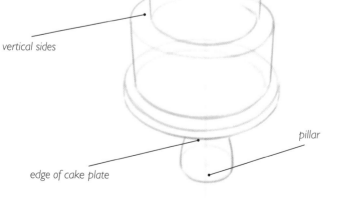

vertical sides

pillar

edge of cake plate

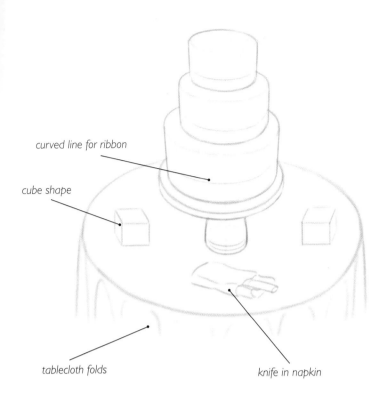

curved line for ribbon

cube shape

tablecloth folds

knife in napkin

Step 3

Define the outline of the cake's form. Add curved lines for ribbon around the middle of each tier and the pillar. For each cube shape, draw a square for the front and then add the top and the sides. Draw an ellipse for the top of the table that disappears behind the cake. Add soft folds around the edges and a napkin and knife on top.

DRAWING TIP

To make something look white, use very light pencil pressure and leave large areas clear. Defining the outline also helps to make the surface look lighter.

Step 4

Draw flowers and leaves cascading down the top of the cake and in the corners of the bottom tier. Use light pencil pressure to shade soft gray shadows down the sides of the cake and for highlights to create shiny ribbons. Build up the gray tone around the pillar. Define the napkin and darken the knife. Once you add glowing candles and shadows around the table, your cake will be ready for cutting!

INTERESTING FACT → Some couples keep a piece of their wedding cake frozen and eat it on their first anniversary.

More Funky Things to Draw—Wedding Day

FIRST DANCE

The first dance is an important moment in a couple's wedding day. It is usually performed after the speeches. The bride and groom embrace, dancing together to a song that symbolizes their love. When their moment in the spotlight is over, the bride may dance with her father or the groom with his mother. After this, the master of ceremonies invites the guests to join them on the dance floor.

Before You Begin

The forms of the bride and groom are built around skeletons. The bride is seen from the back and the groom from the front. A portion of the groom's body is hidden. Their chins and heads are facing each other. Their spines are at the same angle, but the bride is a little shorter.

Step 1

Lightly draw two round heads. The bride's is slightly lower. Add their pointed chins facing each other. Draw the groom's spine, angled shoulders, and chest, and then the bride's. Sketch his hips and overlap hers. Draw his bent leg and a guideline for their feet. Then sketch her skirt with a curved hem below the level of his foot. Sketch his right hand around her back and then draw their outstretched arms, slightly foreshortened, with joined hands. Don't forget the crosses on their faces.

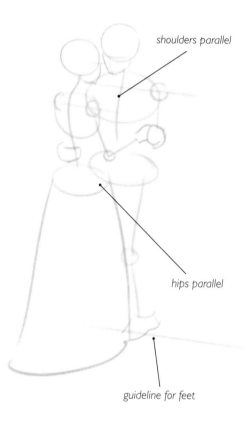

shoulders parallel

hips parallel

guideline for feet

folds of pinned-up train

scalloped hem

Step 2

Build the shape of their forms around the skeletons. Start at the bride's neck, shaping the top of her body and then creating the folds of her dress where her train has been pinned up. Add a wavy hem. Start at the groom's shoulders and shape his jacket and pants.

bun above neckline

fine veil

creases in pants

Step 3

Sketch their hair around their heads, drawing the bride's bun above her neck. Define her facial features and ear. Draw the groom's eyes on either side of the cross and follow with his nose and mouth. Draw his ear and define his face. Define the details of his suit, adding a tie and vest and creases down his outfit. Add fingers to their hand shapes. Define the soft folds of her dress and add a fine transparent veil that hangs to the pinned-up train.

DRAWING TIP

Pretend that you are a wedding dress designer by changing the details of the bride's wedding dress. Perhaps you could make it more lacy or add different jewelry!

Step 4

Using light pencil pressure, add a soft wavy texture to their hair. Shade soft gray tone over their figures and add highlights to their clothing. Add any other details you see. Define their facial features and add her earring. Draw a boutonniere on his lapel. Shade a diagonal shadow under his feet. Once you add the light background of the reception room, your bride and groom will be ready to waltz!

INTERESTING FACT

→ It is not uncommon for the bride and groom to take professional dance lessons before their wedding so they can dance perfectly in front of their family and friends.

More Funky Things to Draw—Wedding Day

WEDDING CAR

The bride and groom may hire a car and driver to take them to the wedding venue or reception. They choose cars that will make a statement of glamour and elegance, such as Bentleys, Rolls Royces, Jaguars, or limousines. The cars often have ribbons attached to their hoods or other decorations. Riding in these beautiful cars adds to the atmosphere of celebration. The cars can also be used as props in the wedding photographs.

Before You Begin

The Rolls Royce wedding car is based around a three-dimensional box shape and is seen from a three-quarter view. Create this drawing carefully by following each step and observing the changes between each stage. Notice that the hood is shaped like a house roof and the wheels are ellipses.

Step 1

Lightly draw an angled box shape that gets narrower at the back. Draw two vertical lines on the front and a triangle above. Add a roof-shaped hood and a curved windshield. Draw a curved side window, leaving a gap for the top of the box shape. Add the car roof. Sketch two ellipses on the side and add curved lines to make the wheels. Draw the bottom of the wheel that hides behind the front corner.

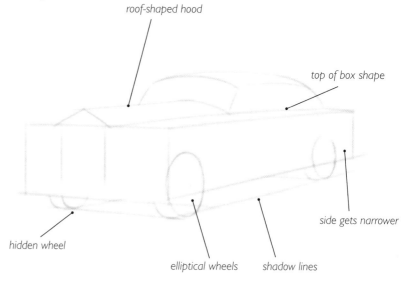

roof-shaped hood

top of box shape

side gets narrower

hidden wheel

elliptical wheels

shadow lines

Step 2

Draw a curved bumper around the front of the box shape. Next, draw curved arches over the wheels and define the rear of the car. Create the curved line of the car's body inside the box shape. Define the windows, roof, and hood. Draw the curved shape of the front of the car inside the box. Define the wheels.

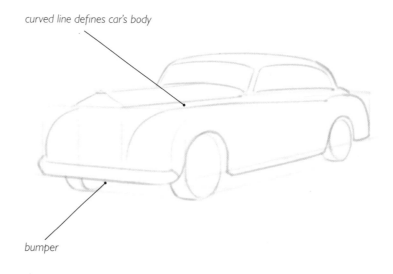

curved line defines car's body

bumper

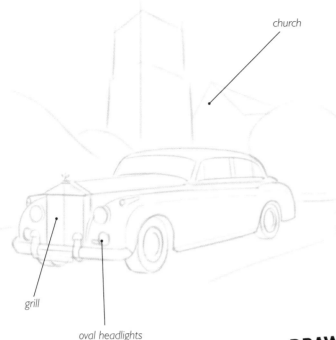

church

grill

oval headlights

Step 3

Lightly draw a wavy road that becomes narrower into the distance. Draw the curved outlines of the trees and add the three-dimensional shapes for the church. Define the grill and add oval headlights on either side. Add curved elements to the bumper. Define the curved form of the car and add detail to the hubcaps.

Step 4

Add ribbon attached to the hood ornament and sketch a vertical line pattern on the grill. With light pencil pressure, shade highlights across the car's body and windows. With medium pencil pressure, build up the darker tone around the front of the car and wheels. Add a shadow underneath. Once you create the details of the church in the background and define the trees, your car will get to the church on time!

DRAWING TIP

Adding shadows can be tricky. Just remember that shadows are softer around the edges and become darker toward the middle.

INTERESTING FACT → Some brides even choose to arrive in a horse-drawn carriage for an old-fashioned or fantasy atmosphere.

More Funky Things to Draw

Dance

Paul Könye • Kate Ashforth

More Funky Things to Draw

Dance

More Funky Things to Draw—Dance

INTRODUCTION

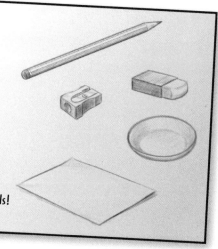

People have been dancing since the birth of human civilization thousands of years ago. In many cultures, people dance during rituals and ceremonies. Modern styles of dance can be linked back to early forms of celebratory and ceremonial dance. For generations, dance has played a strong role in popular culture, and audiences love to be entertained by the dancers' skill and marvel at their beauty. Many dance genres are admired and danced by people around the world.

THINGS YOU WILL NEED

- A gray lead pencil (HB or 2B).
- A pencil sharpener and a dish for shavings.
- Sheets of drawing paper.
- A clean eraser.
- Patience—learning drawing skills takes time and practice.
- Confidence—a positive attitude will help to develop your drawing skills!

Drawing Guidelines

1 There is a process in learning to draw. Follow the steps carefully and in order.
2 Always use light pencil pressure when beginning the first stage of a drawing.
3 If you feel unsure about the instructions, ask an adult for help.
4 Gray lead smudges easily. Pay attention to where your hand is on the page.
5 Clean the gray lead residue off your eraser by rubbing it against a spare piece of paper.
6 Most of the directions for drawing people don't mention the joints of the limbs or the hand and feet shapes, but they're still important! Be sure to draw them in.

Beginner   Intermediate   Expert

The stars at the top of each page grade the difficulty level of each drawing from beginner to intermediate or expert. Some drawings are trickier than others because of the level of detail, but if you carefully follow the basic principles of building a drawing from shapes and lines, you will learn to conquer both simple and complex drawings.

Follow the Steps

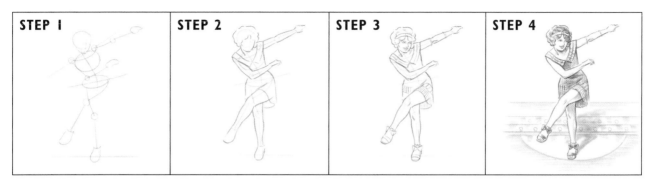

Throughout the following pages, you will find a variety of human subjects. To draw the human form, you need to construct a "skeleton" using a series of joints, lines, and shapes. The form of each subject is shaped around the skeleton using a curved outline. Study the shapes and joints that are drawn for the skeleton and the lengths of all the lines. Observe the line and curve of the spine and the positions and angles of all the body parts.

PENCIL TECHNIQUES FOR DRAWING PEOPLE

The boxes below show three types of shape used for skeletons.

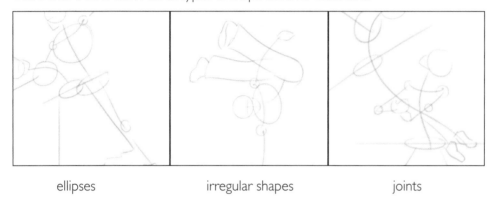

| ellipses | irregular shapes | joints |

When you arrive at each page of this book, observe the types of shapes drawn for each skeleton. Study the size of each shape and look at what part of the body it is used for.

For example, ellipses (flattened ovals) are drawn for hips, and irregular shapes are drawn for legs, feet, and hands. Circles are used for joints such as shoulders and elbows.

Shading and Pencil Pressure

Shading adds detail and definition to a subject. Apply different levels of shading with changes in pencil pressure—a light pencil grip creates a light gray tone, for example.

The boxes below show different levels of gray tone created by a change in pencil pressure.

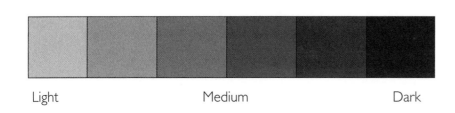

Light   Medium   Dark

More Funky Things to Draw—Dance

BALLROOM DANCING ★ ★ ★

Modern ballroom dancing became prominent in the early 20th century. Social dances called balls were held in halls where people would come to socialize and dance the Viennese waltz, foxtrot, quickstep, modern waltz, and tango. For these dances, a man and a woman take a pose called a "closed hold." In the 1920s, ballroom dancing became so popular that people began to hold competitions, and soon dancing techniques, steps, and music were formalized. Ballroom dance includes dramatic expression of emotion as well as precise technique.

Before You Begin

The ballroom dancers are built around two skeletons that are made up of a series of shapes, joints, lines, and angles. Study the positioning of the elements for each figure so you understand how they connect with each other. Pay attention to where the dancers' heads are facing and where their arms are pointing, as well as how the woman's curved spine is drawn.

Step 1

Lightly draw the man's round head and chin facing to your left. Behind the chin, draw his spine at an angle with an ellipse for the hips. Draw a larger ellipse for his chest. Sketch his straight arm and hand pointing up. Draw a baseline below and sketch the leg in line with his spine and his foot sitting on the baseline. Draw the woman's head and chin facing the man and draw a curve for her spine. Sketch a smaller ellipse for her hips with the skirt shape sitting on the baseline. Draw her open arms and hands.

Step 2

Starting at the man's arm, work your way down both figures drawing the curved outlines of the dancers and the details of their costumes. Draw the woman's foot next to the man's and a curved line for the top edge of the float (extra fabric attached to her dress).

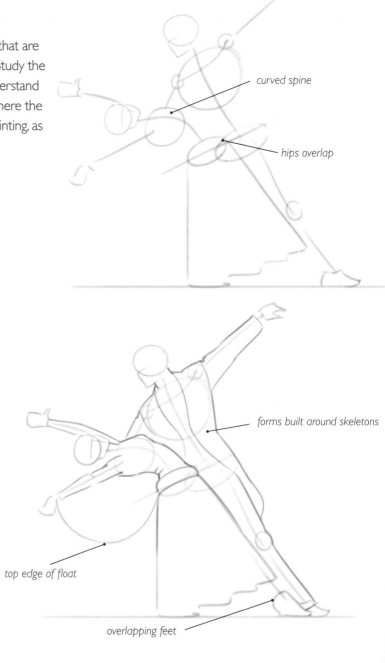

curved spine

hips overlap

forms built around skeletons

top edge of float

overlapping feet

profile

open hands

open hands

float

folds of skirt

Step 3

Inside the hand shapes, draw the open fingers of both dancers. Draw the man's hairline, ear, and hair. Then work your way down the profile of his face. Starting at the arm, create the further details of the man's costume. Sketch the woman's hairline and ear and then draw her eyes, nose, and mouth. Define her arms and create the details of her blouse. On your left, begin drawing each fold of her float and skirt. Above the skirt, add the top of the man's thigh. Don't forget to define both shoes.

Step 4

Starting at the top of the man's arm, use light pencil pressure to shade light gray tone over his hair and suit. For the woman, start shading light gray tone over her arms and work your way down her torso. For the folds, begin at your left and work your way across. Darken and define the outline of both figures and the woman's facial features. Once you finish defining the dancers' shoes, they will be ready to waltz into the night!

INTERESTING FACT → In this context, the term "ball" is derived from the Latin word "ballare," meaning "to dance."

More Funky Things to Draw—Dance

BALLET PAS DE DEUX

Pas de deux is a French term that that means "two people's steps." It is a ballet duet performed by two dancers that involves promenades, jumps, lifts, and pirouettes. In 1796, the French dancer Charles-Louis Didelot produced the ballet Zephyr et Flore, which introduced simple lifts and an intimate, conversational style of pas de deux. During a pas de deux, the man is the stabilizing force, showing off his strength by lifting and turning the woman so she appears to be floating above the stage.

Before You Begin

The ballet dancers are built around two skeletons. Observe the angles at the joints and the length of each body part. Pay close attention to the curve in the female dancer's spine and the distance between her head and her feet, while the male dancer is crossing his arms and holding her at the knees.

Step 1

Lightly sketch the woman's head at a slight angle, drawing the long curve of her spine and top leg. Draw her oval chest, adding open arms and hands. Sketch her tilted hips and a straight guideline across her foot. Draw her shorter leg with her foot under the guideline. Draw the man's head and chin facing up. Add a spine curving down to his hips at the guideline. Draw shoulders and his arms crossing over her knees. Sketch his legs with the feet on the baseline.

Step 2

Build the dancers' outlines around their skeletons. Starting at the woman's top arm, draw her curved chest, her other arm, and her legs. Draw her skirt and the male dancer's arms. Next, draw his outline from head to toe and add face crosses.

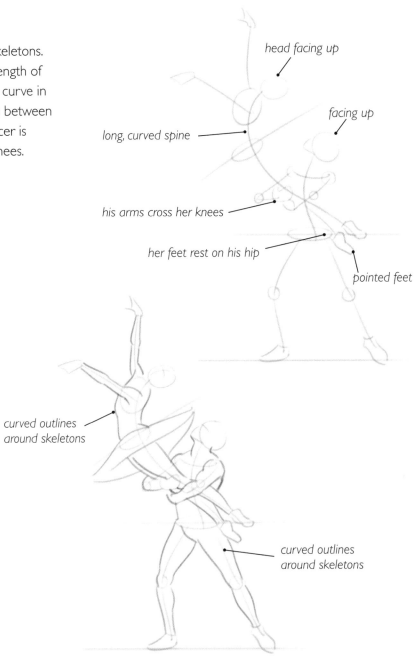

head facing up

facing up

long, curved spine

his arms cross her knees

her feet rest on his hip

pointed feet

curved outlines around skeletons

curved outlines around skeletons

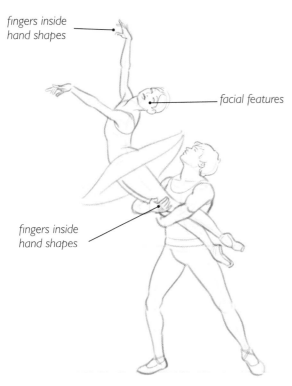

fingers inside
hand shapes

facial features

fingers inside
hand shapes

Step 3

Draw both dancers' fingers inside the hand shapes. Outline their hair and add their ears. Turn your page around to draw the woman's eyes, nose, and mouth over the cross and define her jaw and neck. Now draw the man's profile in the same order. Define his elbow and costume. Add the details for their ballet shoes.

DRAWING TIP

Don't forget to erase any unwanted line work as you go. Make sure your eraser is clean!

Step 4

Study the soft shading and fine details over each dancer's form. Using light pencil pressure, start at her top arm and work your way down both of their figures, adding shading and details as you go. Build up the darker shadows under their limbs and add her tiara. Once you define their facial features and add texture for their hair, your dancers will be ready to perform a pas de deux!

INTERESTING FACT → Italian dancer Marie Taglioni created the puffy, white tulle skirt that became a standard hallmark for a ballerina.

BREAK DANCER

Break dancing is a style of street dance that originated in New York in the 1970s. During the 1980s, break dancing moved off the streets and into the world of popular culture when African-American youth began breaking in music videos and movies, showing off their flashy, acrobatic, and highly technical moves. Breakers often wear comfortable street clothes such as baggy shirts and loose pants. Hip hop music is the most common soundtrack for breaking, and each dancer creates their own choreography.

Before You Begin

The break dancer is built using a series of different shapes that are connected by the spine, collarbone, and arms. The collarbone, bottom arm, and head are all vertically aligned. The cross on the face is in line with the top of the spine. Notice the perspective: the front leg is shorter than the back leg and the shoes are different sizes.

Step 1

Lightly draw a round head with a round chin pointing to your right. Overlapping the chin, draw an oval for the chest and sketch a curved collarbone. Add a cross to the face and draw the curved spine. Sketch the top leg and foot at an angle. Then draw a baseline underneath. Add shoulder joints and extend a line for the bottom arm down to the baseline. Draw a line for the top arm overlapping the leg, and sketch both hand shapes. Next, draw the back leg parallel with the baseline.

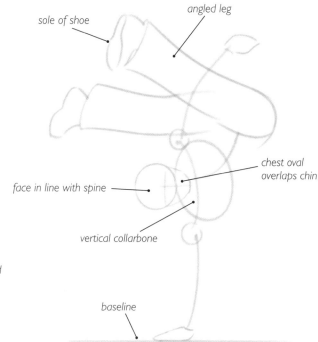

sole of shoe

angled leg

chest oval overlaps chin

face in line with spine

vertical collarbone

baseline

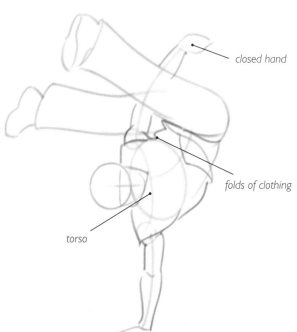

closed hand

folds of clothing

torso

Step 2

Build the curved form of the dancer around the shapes and construction lines. Start at the top arm and work your way down the body, concentrating on the folds of clothing.

face over cross

folds in jeans

Step 3

Create the details of the hands and shoes. Lightly draw the folds of the jeans and draw the fuzzy outline of the hair around the head. Turn your page around to draw eyes on either side of the cross, followed by the nose and mouth. Sketch the headband around the forehead and define the ears and neck. Erase any line work you no longer need.

DRAWING TIP

Carefully follow the instructions in order. They're designed to make it easier for you to draw a subject correctly.

Step 4

Add the details to the shoes and define the facial features. Using light pencil pressure, begin at the top of the figure and add light gray shading over the whole body. Concentrate on adding darker shadowing around the hips, the top shoe, and the neck and hair. Once you draw the dancer in the background and the graffiti wall, your b-boy will be ready to break!

INTERESTING FACT ➡ Friends and rivals frequently compete in break dancing battles (dance competitions), performing solo or in crews.

More Funky Things to Draw—Dance

BOLLYWOOD DANCER

Bollywood dance is a high-energy style that appears in movies made in Bollywood, a nickname for the film industry in Mumbai, India (formerly called Bombay). Bollywood films have become popular around the world because of their lavish productions and musical dance scenes, often featuring dozens of dancers performing synchronized moves. The dance movements are part of the extravaganza, fusing traditional Indian folk dance and international styles of hip hop.

Before You Begin

The Bollywood dancer's form is built around a skeleton for the torso and thick cylindrical shapes for the legs. The dancer's hips face to your left, while her torso is turned toward the front. Draw the front leg shape before the back leg shape to achieve the correct pose, and keep the spine aligned with the back leg.

Step 1

Lightly draw a round head with a pointed chin turned slightly to your left. Draw the spine from the back of the chin, curving down. Add a chest oval with a curved collarbone at the top. Draw shoulder joints and the angled arm to your left, pointing up. Add a curved hand shape. Sketch the front leg and then add the back leg in line with the spine. Draw a baseline, with the feet sitting on top. Draw the other arm with the flattened hand shape over the hip.

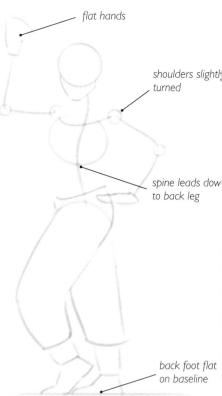

flat hands

shoulders slightl turned

spine leads dow to back leg

back foot flat on baseline

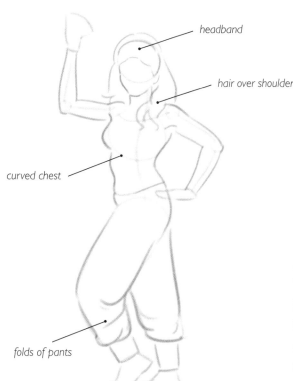

headband

hair over shoulder

curved chest

folds of pants

Step 2

Build the curved form of the dancer around the skeleton. Draw the outlines for both the arms and follow with the chest. Define her shoulders, neck, and face. Draw a curve around the top of her head with wavy hair falling around the shoulders. Define the folds of her pants.

spread fingers

face over cross

Step 3

Draw the face cross. Add eyes on either side of the cross, followed by the nose and the smiling mouth. Draw the details of the head jewels, earrings, necklace, and armbands. Draw her top and add fingers to the hand shapes. Further define the folds of the pants, and add details for her shoes and the line pattern in her hair.

DRAWING TIP

To make something light-colored look three-dimensional, leave most of the area white and lightly shade highlights in gray tone.

Step 4

Study the different levels of gray tone over the dancer's form. Starting with her raised arm, use a light pencil grip to softly shade her skin, the folds in her pants, and her shoes. Define and darken the details of her face. Draw her pupils, her hair, and bands around her pants. Then darken the texture of her hair. Once you draw the Bollywood scene in the background, your dancer will be ready for her starring role!

INTERESTING FACT → Australian director Baz Lurhmann drew on Bollywood film productions for inspiration when making the film *Moulin Rouge*.

More Funky Things to Draw—Dance

THE CHARLESTON

The Charleston dance became popular in the early 1900s. The dance originated in an African-American community living on a small island near Charleston, South Carolina. The Charleston is performed in a quick 4/4 rhythm. The feet move back and forward in swift kicks while the arms swing. Little hops and rotations of the hands are included in between steps. In the early 1920s the Charleston was introduced into mainstream theater in New York, and the dance became an instant hit and a signature dance of that period.

Before You Begin

Before you draw the Charleston dancer's shoulders and hips, lightly sketch the guidelines so you draw them at the correct angles. Her spine is foreshortened and her head and arms are pointing in the same direction. Also, pay attention to how the overlapping legs are drawn.

Step 1

Lightly draw a round head with a pointed chin turned to your right. Draw a facial cross that faces to your right. Sketch a guideline underneath, drawing a round chest over the top. Draw a foreshortened spine, sketching a guideline at the hips with an ellipse over the top. Sketch a collarbone over the chest with the arms pointing to your right. The front arm crosses over the spine and hips. Next, draw a baseline. Sketch the dancer's straight leg and foot sitting over the baseline. Cross the other leg over the thigh, with the foot above the line.

Step 2

Draw the outline of the dancer's wavy hair around her head. Draw a line for her neck and her shoulders above her jaw. Draw a V shape for her collar and form her arms, torso, and hips around the skeleton. Form her top leg and drape her skirt over the thigh. Form her bottom leg and draw fingers inside the hand shapes.

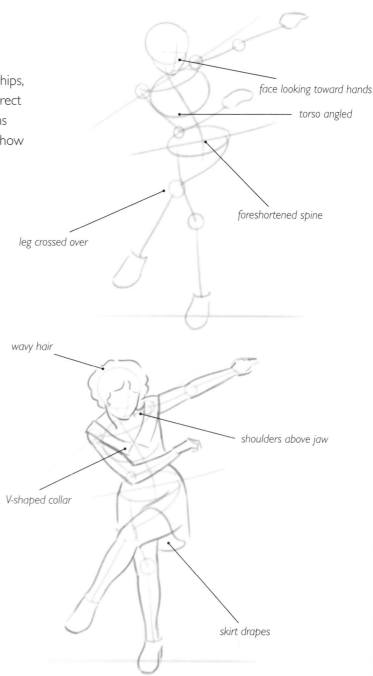

face looking toward hands

torso angled

foreshortened spine

leg crossed over

wavy hair

shoulders above jaw

V-shaped collar

skirt drapes

eyes look to your right

line pattern fans out

Step 3

Draw the dancer's eyes, nose, and open mouth over the cross. Draw her pupils looking to your right. Sketch a headband above her bangs and add texture to her hair. Add a line inside her collar and add details to her arms. Draw bangles and a line pattern fanning around the band of her hemline. Define her knees and add bows to her ankles. Finish her shoes.

DRAWING TIP

An easy way to remember what 'horizontal' means is to think of the horizon line.

Step 4

With medium pencil pressure, add wavy, darker shading to her hair and vertical shading to the body of her dress. Add a circular pattern to her collar and to the band of her hemline. Define the pleated outline of her hem. Darken her shoes and her facial features. With a light pencil grip, shade light gray tone over the edges of her skin. Once you draw the stage in the background and the dancer's shadow, your dancer will be ready to swing!

INTERESTING FACT → Women who enjoyed dancing the Charleston were called flappers because they flapped their arms like birds.

More Funky Things to Draw—Dance

THE TANGO

The tango is a close dance that originated in Buenos Aires, Argentina, and Montevideo, Uruguay, in the late 1800s. Couples embrace each other in an open or closed hold, with their hips and chests close, and engage in a series of dramatic moves and rhythmic steps. The origins of the name aren't known for sure, but it may be from an African language. Argentina is a melting pot of different cultures that influence one another's music and dance.

Before You Begin

The dancers' forms are built around two skeletons. Make sure to position their heads, hands, and legs correctly. You will observe that the dancers' legs overlap. Also, pay close attention to the ways their chests and arms are joined.

Step 1

Lightly draw both dancers' round heads at a slight angle, with their chins close together. Draw their curved spines from behind their chins. Sketch the man's chest and then slightly overlap the woman's smaller chest. Sketch the woman's arm across the man's chest. Draw the man's sharply angled arm. Notice how their hands are connected. Draw slightly angled ellipses for their hips. Underneath, draw two baselines at different angles. Sketch the man's legs, positioning his feet on his baseline. Overlap the woman's legs, drawing her feet on her baseline.

Step 2

Build the curved outlines of the dancers around their skeletons. Starting at the woman's neck, gradually work your way down to her feet, drawing the form of her body. Use the same process to draw the man's form. Draw crosses over their faces.

facing each other

hands connected

chests touch

legs overlap

two baselines

hand cups shoulder blade

outlines around skeletons

facing each other

hem just above knees

Step 3

Draw the woman's hair and then the man's. Next, draw their hairlines and ears. Sketch the woman's profile and define her dress. Draw a double hemline just above her knees. Draw the man's facial features using the lines of the facial cross. Draw the details of his suit. Draw his fingers inside the hand shapes and define both dancers' shoes.

DRAWING TIP

When drawing soft patterns or textures, make sure your pencil is not too sharp and angle it rather than using the point.

Step 4

Study the different levels of gray tone over the dancers' bodies. Using light pencil pressure, shade light gray tone over the man's clothing, building up the darker areas of tone as you go. Follow the same process for the woman's skin and dress. Add the soft points of material over her hemline. Define and darken their facial features. Once you darken the man's hair and their shoes and sketch in the courtyard, your dancers will be ready to tango!

INTERESTING FACT

→ In 2009, Argentina and Uruguay successfully petitioned UNESCO to have the tango be declared an important part of the world's cultural heritage.

More Funky Things to Draw—Dance

TAP DANCER ⭐ ⭐

Tap dancing is a theatrical style of dance developed in America during the 1800s, influenced by a variety of dances from African, Scottish, English, and Irish cultures. Tap dancers tap out rhythms on the floor with their shoes, which have hard plates on the soles, while dancing, jumping, and twirling acrobatically. Tap first became popular during the vaudeville era. In the early 20th century, movie stars like Fred Astaire and Gene Kelly built their careers on the art of dancing tap.

Before You Begin

The tap dancer is built around a skeleton made up of a series of shapes and construction lines. To achieve the right perspective, you must draw the head, shoulders, and hips at the correct angles. Pay close attention to how the spine curves around from the middle of the collarbone, and to the head facing to your left.

Step 1

Lightly draw a small circle for the head with a chin underneath. Then add a facial cross facing to your left. Sketch a sharply angled line for the collarbone, and starting from the middle of the collarbone, add the curved spine. Draw bent lines for arms, one overlapping the spine and the other pointing upward. Add joints and hands. Sketch round shapes for the chest and hip area and draw a baseline on a slight angle. Draw the legs, sketching the feet on the baseline.

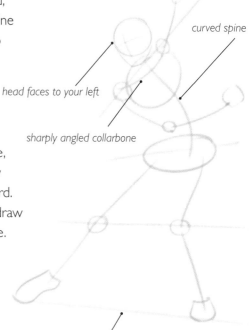

curved spine

head faces to your left

sharply angled collarbone

baseline

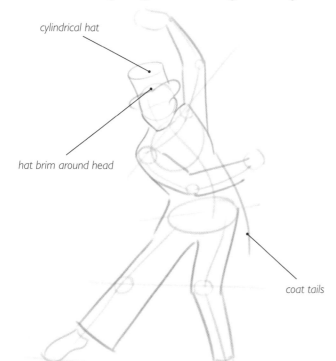

cylindrical hat

hat brim around head

coat tails

Step 2

Draw a line for the hat's brim around the head and add a cylinder for the top hat. Define and darken the outline of the head and shoulders. Build the form of the arms and torso around the construction lines. Draw a line for the coat and shape the legs.

Step 3

Inside the top hand shape, draw fingers. Then create the folds of the sleeve. Repeat this process for the second arm and add a cane to the hand. Define the curved outline of the jacket and pants. Draw the shoes, bowtie, and flower. Draw the facial features over the cross and another line across the hat brim.

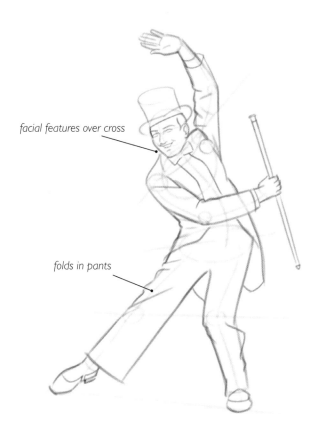

facial features over cross

folds in pants

DRAWING TIP

Folds in fabric are achieved by applying gray tone around the edge of a fold. On top of the fold, leave a white area to make it look like light is hitting that area.

Step 4

Study the different levels of shading over the whole body. Starting at the top hand, shade lightly down the sleeves, jacket, and pants. Observe how the folds of the suit are slightly darker. Build up darker levels of shading under the arms, and on the jacket and shoes. Once you define the face and cane and add an elliptical stage, your dancer will be ready to tap!

INTERESTING FACT → In the early years of tap dancing, percussive sounds were made with instruments. It wasn't until the 1920s that taps were put on the bottom of shoes!

More Funky Things to Draw—Dance

BALINESE DANCER

Bali is an island that is part of the country of Indonesia. Balinese dance plays an important role in celebrations and Hindu religious ceremonies. Since the beginning of Balinese history, people have acted out dramatic stories inspired by Hindu mythology. Typically, Balinese dancers wear colorful and ornate traditional headpieces and dresses. They perform with their legs half-bent, swaying their torsos from side to side, and raise and lower their arms in gestures that display supple movements of their hands and fingers.

Before You Begin

The Balinese dancer's feet are anchored to the ground. Her curved skirt and spine are what give her a sense of movement. The positioning of her hips, arms, and face make her look as though she is moving from side to side. Pay attention to the decorative elements that are added in step 3.

Step 1

Lightly draw a round head with a chin pointing to your left. Add a line for eyes. Draw a curved spine with an angled ellipse for the hips. Add a round chest with a collarbone across the top. Sketch a curved shape for the skirt that makes the dancer's legs look bent. Below, sketch the front foot in line with the spine and the other foot pointing to your right. Draw arms with elbows pointing outward and one hand over the spine.

Step 2

Draw a pointed headpiece curving around the top of the skull and a fringe below. Build the rest of the dancer's form around the skeleton. Define her head, neck, and ear. Next, shape the arm, chest, and skirt. Draw lines across the chest and waist for the details of her costume. Draw a vertical line for the opening of the skirt. Sketch a fan shape over the arm on your right with a fringe hanging down. Shape the rest of the arm.

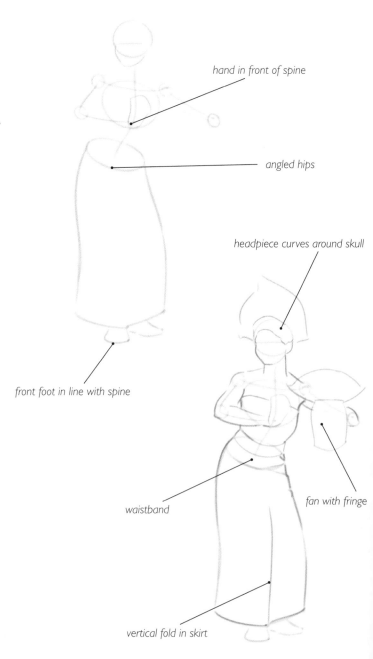

hand in front of spine

angled hips

headpiece curves around skull

front foot in line with spine

waistband

fan with fringe

vertical fold in skirt

Step 3

Erase any lines you no longer need. Sketch details around the headpiece and add a choker around the dancer's neck. Draw eyes across the guideline and add her nose and mouth. Add a circle to the waistband with two sashes hanging down. Define her fingers inside the hand shape and add a bangle to her wrist. Draw diagonal lines across her costume. Define her feet inside the shapes and add leaf shapes across the top of the fan. Add rosettes and shredded material hanging down. Shape the arm around the fan.

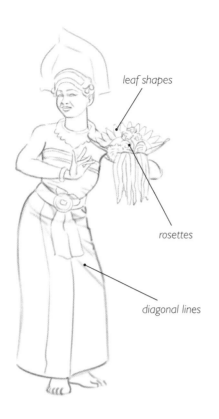

leaf shapes

rosettes

diagonal lines

DRAWING TIP

Remember that your eyes are your best tools! Use them with confidence to carefully observe the fine details, textures, and patterns that are added to a drawing.

Step 4

For the headpiece, draw fringing around the edge and add a soft texture to the center and a pattern around the band. Add pattern to the choker and bangle. Using light pencil pressure, work your way down the body, shading gray diagonal lines and folds over the costume. Notice that some areas are left white. Define and darken the dancer's facial features and fan. Once you shade the shadow around her feet and softly sketch the temple garden in the background, your Balinese dancer will be ready to sway!

INTERESTING FACT

→ One of the most popular Balinese dances is a dance of welcome called Panyembrama. At the end of the dance, the dancers sprinkle their guests with flower petals.

More Funky Things to Draw—Dance

DISCO DANCERS

The birth of disco dates back to the early 1970s, when DJs began playing records live in clubs. Clubs started using mirror balls and flickering multi-colored lights, and flashy satin and sequined clothing and big hair became fashionable. Disco's musical influences came from soul, blues, funk, and rock, and new dancing styles were created to match the soaring sound effects and intense vocals. Disco dance incorporates sleek turns, jumps, lifts, heel clicking, and rhythmic forward and back movements.

Before You Begin

The disco dancers' bodies are built around skeletons. To achieve the correct poses for the dancers, pay attention to the height of their arms, the angles of their hips, and how the woman's feet are in front of the man's. Also, notice that the dancers face each other and are different heights.

Step 1

Lightly draw two round heads a distance apart and at two different heights. Draw pointed chins facing the center of the drawing. Sketch both dancers' spines. Draw two angled ellipses for hips. Sketch a big chest for the man and a smaller one for the woman, both slightly angled. Draw her short collarbone and his longer one. Draw her top arm in line with her head and her front arm over her hips. Sketch his arm behind her waist and his other arm opening out. Draw two baselines underneath. Draw the woman's feet sitting on the front baseline. Sketch the man's legs behind, making sure their legs overlap.

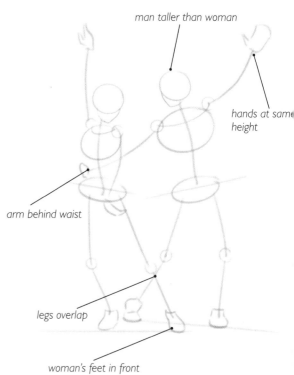

man taller than woman

hands at same height

arm behind waist

legs overlap

woman's feet in front

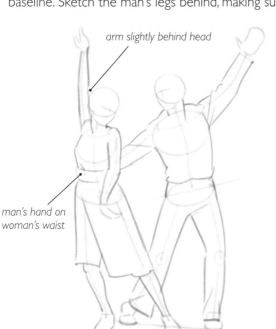

arm slightly behind head

man's hand on woman's waist

Step 2

Build the dancers' forms around the skeletons. Starting at the woman's top hand, work your way down her body, shaping her curved outline as you go. Follow the same process for the man. Observe that his arm now disappears behind the woman and a small part of his hand is seen at her waist. Add facial crosses.

wavy hair

wavy hair

erase construction lines

Step 3

Draw a wavy outline for the woman's hair around her head, shoulders, and face. Sketch her eyes, nose, and mouth over the cross. Follow the same process for the man. Draw fingers inside all of the hand shapes. Start at their shoulders and work your way down, adding the details of their clothing and shoes. Define and darken their outlines and erase any lines you no longer need.

DRAWING TIP

To draw a checked floor pattern in perspective, draw the squares smaller and closer together at the top and larger and more open at the bottom.

Step 4

Using light pencil pressure, work your way down the dancers' bodies, adding light shading to their skin and the folds of their clothing. Build up the darker texture of their wavy hair and darken their shoes. Define their facial features. Starting at the top of the stage, draw the soft checked pattern of the dance floor under the dancers' feet. Once you draw a mirror ball overhead, your disco dancers will be ready to hustle!

INTERESTING FACT → The 1977 film *Saturday Night Fever* portrays the competitive disco dancing movement. The soundtrack, featuring the hit single "Stayin' Alive" by the Bee Gees, is the best-selling soundtrack of all time.

More Funky Things to Draw—Dance

CONTEMPORARY DANCE

Contemporary dance is a name given to a series of modern dancing styles. The choreography of contemporary dance is interpretive and often full of emotion. Where many dance genres focus on excellence in technique and structured steps, contemporary dance is expressive, free-flowing, and unconventional. Contemporary dance was developed in the early 1900s by Isadora Duncan and Martha Graham, who rebelled against the rules of ballet and opened up an entirely new world of movement.

Before You Begin

The dancer is seen leaping in profile. In step 2, the position of the body almost looks flat, with the legs opened outward and the chest and hip area curved back. Pay special attention to the way the head arches back, the back leg pointing up over the head, and the arch of the spine.

Step 1

Lightly draw a round head with a chin shape pointing up and to your right. Next, draw a short, curved spine and add a round chest in the middle. For hips, sketch a flattened diamond shape at the base of the spine. Draw a sharp angled line for the back leg pointing up behind the dancer, and a straight leg on the opposite side. Draw the feet and add a baseline far below. From the neck, draw a line for the arm overlapping the head and the knee, and add a pointed hand shape.

Step 2

Build the form of the dancer around the skeleton. Starting at the neck, draw the curved outline of the chest, arm, straight leg, and bent back leg.

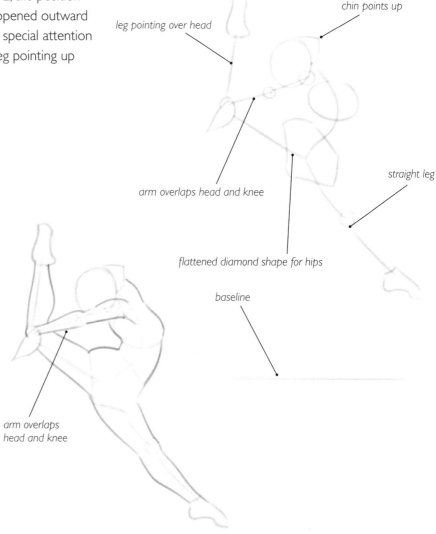

leg pointing over head

chin points up

arm overlaps head and knee

straight leg

flattened diamond shape for hips

baseline

arm overlaps head and knee

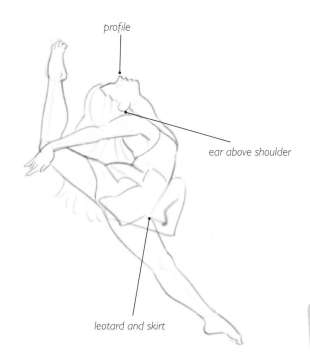

profile

ear above shoulder

leotard and skirt

Step 3

Define the forehead around the head circle, and turn the page around to draw the dancer's profile. Draw the top of the leotard. Starting at the back leg, draw the folds of the skirt. Add pointed fingers and toes to the hand and feet. Draw the dancer's hairline and ear around the forehead, and the wavy lines of her long hair behind.

DRAWING TIP

When a subject has a tilted head, turn your page around so you can draw the face from a vertical position.

Step 4

Define and darken the outline of the dancer's form. Draw the eye, brow, and details of the ear. Starting at the neck, use light pencil pressure to shade gray shadows around the neck, arm, and legs. Build up darker levels of tone under the arm and in the folds of her costume. Once you create the darker shading for her hair and the stage set, your dancer will be ready to leap!

INTERESTING FACT → In recent years, contemporary dancers have borrowed moves from exercise styles like yoga and pilates.

More Funky Things to Draw

Birds

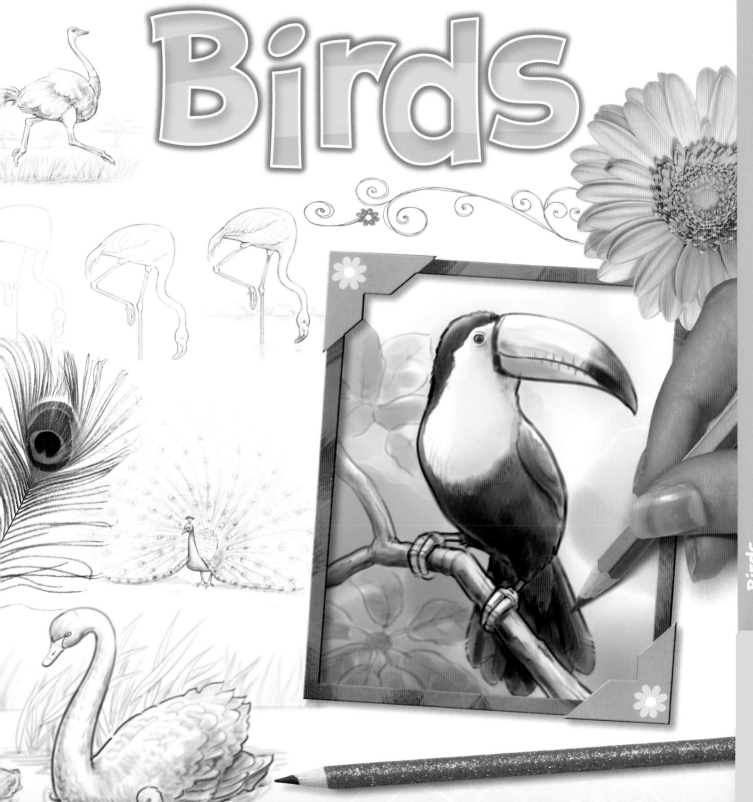

Paul Könye • Kate Ashforth

More Funky Things to Draw

Birds

INTRODUCTION

Birds evolved from reptiles around 150 million years ago. They are very accomplished animals that live in all parts of the world, traveling for food and favorable weather conditions. Humans have long admired them for their attractive appearance and fascinating behavior. Throughout history, people have hunted birds for their brilliant and colorful plumage and studied them to learn the secrets of flight.

THINGS YOU WILL NEED

- A gray lead pencil (HB or 2B).
- A pencil sharpener and a dish for shavings.
- Sheets of drawing paper.
- A clean eraser.
- Patience—learning drawing skills takes time and practice.
- Confidence—a positive attitude will help to develop your drawing skills!

Drawing Guidelines

1 There is a process in learning to draw. Follow the steps carefully and in order.
2 Always use light pencil pressure when beginning the first stage of a drawing.
3 If you feel unsure about the instructions, ask an adult for help.
4 Gray lead smudges easily. Pay attention to where your hand is on the page.
5 Clean the gray lead residue off your eraser by rubbing it against a spare piece of paper.

Beginner   Intermediate   Expert

The stars at the top of each page grade the difficulty level of each drawing from beginner to intermediate or expert. Some drawings are trickier than others because of the level of detail, but if you carefully follow the basic principles of building a drawing from shapes and lines, you will learn to conquer both simple and complex drawings.

Follow the Steps

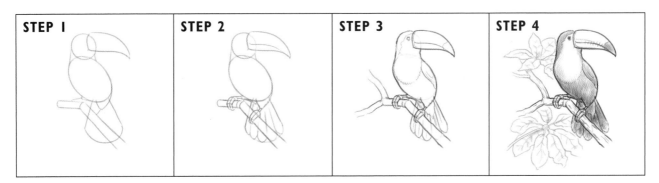

Study the changes between each step and the pencil techniques used. You will notice that birds are drawn using a series of rounded and irregular shapes and different types of line. Feathers and shading are applied in the final steps.

PENCIL TECHNIQUES

The boxes below show three types of pencil work.

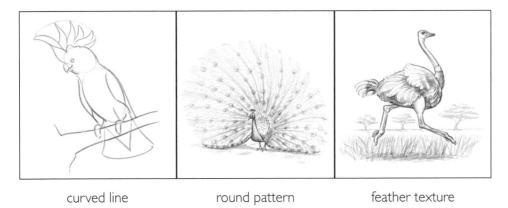

| curved line | round pattern | feather texture |

Observe the types of marks that are applied for each subject. Are they thick, wavy, or fine? Are they soft, dark, or rounded? Before you begin, try experimenting with the different pencil techniques on a separate piece of paper.

Shading and Pencil Pressure

Shading adds detail and definition to a subject. Apply different levels of shading with changes in pencil pressure—a light pencil grip creates a light gray tone, for example.

The boxes below show different levels of gray tone created by a pencil.

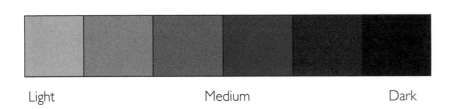

Light   Medium   Dark

More Funky Things to Draw—Birds

TOUCAN ⭐ ⭐

Toucans are remarkable birds that live in the jungle treetops of Central and South America. Other animals can find them very intimidating because of their big bills, which are made from a light, spongy tissue called keratin, and their colorful plumage. A toucan will use its bill to reach for fruit, or extend it into tree trunks to rummage for food. The toucan does not sing like other bird species: it makes a harsh croaking sound that can be heard from miles away.

Before You Begin

The toucan is created out of a series of rounded shapes for the head, body, and tail. It is important to pay attention to the positioning of the beak and tail. Also, observe the angle of the body and how the bird's feet are perched on the branch. This will help you draw the toucan in the right perspective.

Step 1

Observe the different-sized shapes drawn for each part of the body. Lightly sketch a circle for the head and draw the bill shape straight out to the bird's left (your right). Draw a curved point on the end of the bill. Directly under the head, sketch an egg shape on an angle for the body. Draw two lines on an angle for the bent branch. Sketch a fan shape for the tail over the branch.

Step 2

Note the angle of the legs and feet and where they are positioned on the branch. Draw one leg at the top of the branch and the other in the middle. Then attach the feet. Next, sketch a line pattern for the tail feathers behind the branch. Add a curved line to the bill for the mouth and a line detail to the branch.

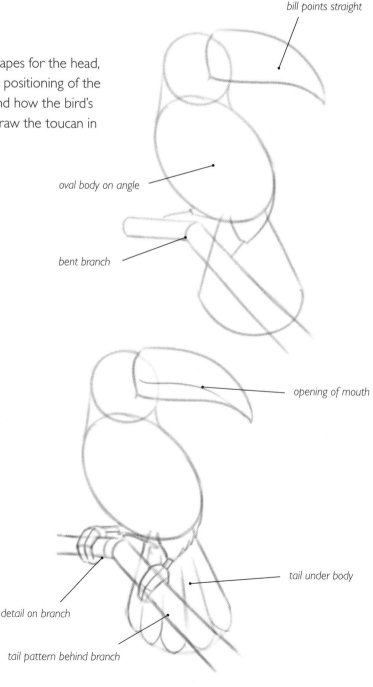

bill points straight

oval body on angle

bent branch

opening of mouth

tail under body

detail on branch

tail pattern behind branch

curved outline around shapes

curved line of feathers

feather detail around leg

Step 3

Create the curved outline of the toucan around the shapes. Note how the pencil line is darker. Sketch a circle for the eye with lines around it. Draw a wing shape curving down the bird's left side. Add a soft, curved line of feathers to the head and chest area, and a curved line around the bill. Add feather patterns inside the tail and marks across the claws. Sketch a fork at the end of the tree branch.

Step 4

With medium pencil pressure, shade tone across the toucan's plumage, eye, and bill. Draw more fine feather details inside the tail. Sketch a pattern on the bill that looks like stitching. Lightly draw the leaves in the background. Once you add texture for the bark, your toucan will be looking for fruit!

DRAWING TIP

Before you begin copying something, pay attention to the different shapes you will be sketching. This will allow you to create a well-balanced drawing.

INTERESTING FACT → A toucan's flexible tail vertebrae allow it to snap its tail forward over its head, and toucans can often be found sleeping in this position!

DOVE ⭐

Doves are beautiful birds. In the Biblical story of Noah, a dove was sent from the ark, across the sea to find land. When it returned with an olive branch, Noah knew that land was near. A famous Spanish painter named Pablo Picasso designed a logo inspired by this story for the International Peace Congress in Paris in 1949. His simple black-line artwork of a dove with an olive branch has popularized the dove as an international symbol of peace.

Before You Begin

Pay particular attention to the size of the body shapes, the fan-shaped tail, and the positions of both wings. Note that the dove's left wing (on your right) is smaller and is on top of the body. The right wing is larger and to the side. This makes the smaller wing look like it is further away.

Step 1

Draw lightly at first. Sketch a larger oval for the chest on a slight angle. Overlap a smaller oval for the head. Connect the body shape to the chest. Draw the body on a slight angle, pointing down to the left. Add a fan-shaped tail to the point. Sketch the smaller, curved wing on top of the body, pointing up. Now add the larger, leaf-shaped wing on the left side of the body.

Step 2

Define and smooth the curved outline of the dove around the shapes. Concentrate on the curvy line work around the chest and onto the tail. Add muscular forms to the wings using lines. Note that the muscle of the left wing extends onto the chest area. Now draw the feet, sharp beak, and eye.

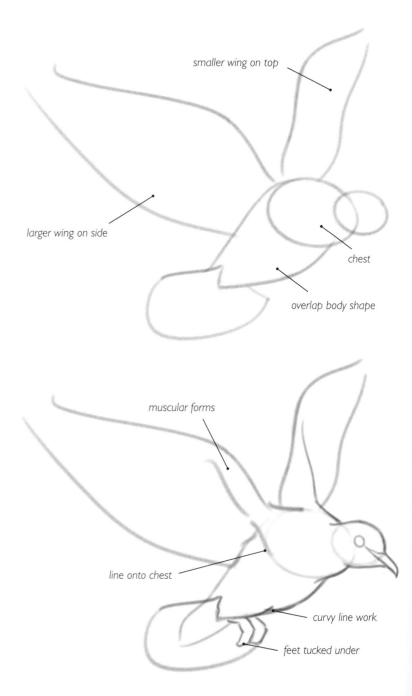

smaller wing on top

larger wing on side

chest

overlap body shape

muscular forms

line onto chest

curvy line work

feet tucked under

space near muscle

bumpy outline

line pattern

Step 3

Starting from the top of the left wing, draw the line pattern for the feathers, leaving a space near the muscle. Continue with the right wing. Define the bumpy outline of each wing. Follow the same process for the fan-shaped tail. Sketch in the claws for the feet.

Step 4

Study the level of shading around the edges of the body, wings, and tail. With light pencil pressure, create the soft shading. Add further details to the left wing. Once you sketch the olive branch in the dove's beak, it will be ready to take flight to help make peace.

DRAWING TIP

If you want to learn to draw circles, ovals, or ellipses well, practice by drawing them over and over again. With a gray lead pencil, using a light pencil grip, quickly rotate your hand in a circular motion as you sketch across the page.

INTERESTING FACT → White doves are often used for magic tricks, as they are intelligent creatures that are easy to teach.

EMPEROR PENGUIN

Emperor penguins are the largest of their species and have breeding habits that are most unusual. During the winter months, the female lays one egg and then travels out to sea, to return in the springtime. The male is left to incubate the egg under his pouch of feathery skin, which protects it from the extreme Antarctic conditions. He keeps warm by huddling with other males from his colony and they all fast until the females return.

Before You Begin

Study the irregular shapes used to construct the body of the emperor penguin and chick. Pay attention to how the adult penguin's head bends over to the left and the chick's head points upward. In step 4, note that the shading across the penguin is a medium to dark level of tone.

Step 1

Lightly draw the adult penguin's head and chest line. Sketch a baseline underneath. Draw a line for the backbone from the top of the head, curving around to the baseline. Now add a sharp beak to the bottom of the head. Next, draw a circle for the chick's head above the baseline. Add curved lines for its back and chest, and a sharp open beak pointing up.

Step 2

Define and darken the penguins' outlines. Add the curved outlines for both wings and the flippers under each penguin. With a clean eraser, remove the line work you no longer need.

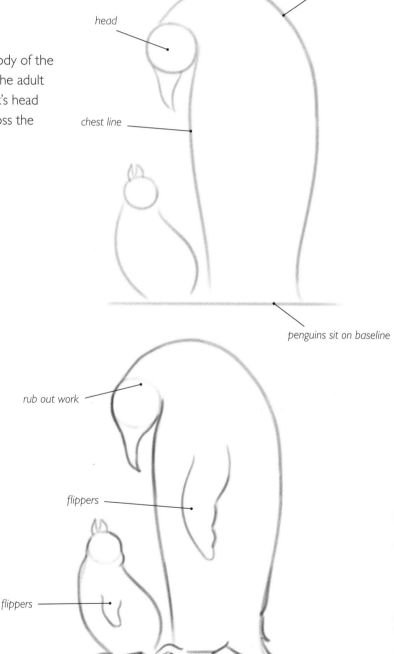

line inside beak

DRAWING TIP

If you begin sketching with a light pencil pressure, it will be easier to remove any line work or shading you no longer want, using a clean eraser.

Step 3

Draw the adult penguin's eye looking down and the chick's looking up. Add a line inside the chick's beak and the opening of the adult's beak. Starting at the head, lightly draw the curved lines and feathery marks over both penguins.

Step 4

With medium pencil pressure, shade a dark tone across the heads of both penguins. Shade a light to medium gray tone across the adult penguin from the back of the neck, darkening it around the wing and flippers. Using a light pencil grip, shade the softer tones around the edges of each penguin. Once you add a shadow under the birds, and rocks to the icy background, your penguins will be ready to waddle!

INTERESTING FACT → Emperor penguins can dive to a depth of 1740 feet and remain underwater for 20 minutes.

More Funky Things to Draw—Birds

CARDINAL

Cardinal birds inhabit the Americas. The male cardinal is a striking crimson color and has a black throat and red bill. Cardinals are songbirds, and their distinctive whistling sound can be heard coming from the treetops. They sing in clear song patterns that are repeated several times over, and make a short chirping sound when predators are near.

Before You Begin

It is important to pay attention to the angle of the branch and the positions of the cardinal's head, feet, and tail. This will help you draw the cardinal in the correct perspective. Also, note where the head sits on the body shape and how the line of the wing extends from the crest down to the wing tip.

Step 1

Lightly sketch the round body on a slight angle, adding a circle for the head. Sketch the branch on an angle below the body. For the head, overlap the circle with a triangular beak and draw the crest on top. Add the line that contours the neck and extend the wing over the body. Draw the tail shape pointing outward. Then draw the legs and feet over the branch.

Step 2

Define and smooth the outline of the cardinal, adding bumpy outlines for the head and wing. Add the opening for the mouth on the beak and draw the circle for the eye. Create the soft, feathery marks around the head, chest, and tail area. Draw the line work inside the tail, and define the legs and claws.

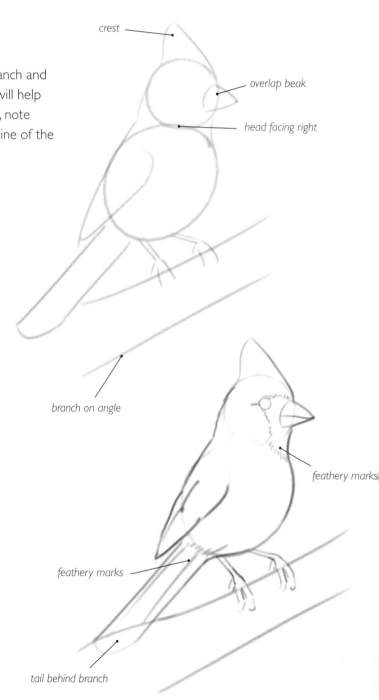

crest

overlap beak

head facing right

branch on angle

feathery marks

feathery marks

tail behind branch

I

Step 3

Using medium pencil pressure, build up a darker level of tone for the shading across the face area. With light pencil pressure, create the soft line work and shading for the feathers on the crest and lower part of the bird's body. Next, draw the soft, puffy outline of the snow around the feet. Once you draw the rest of the branch and add a bark pattern for texture, your cardinal is ready to sing!

DRAWING TIP

When sharpening your pencil, always have a dish next to you to empty pencil shavings into. That way you won't have to keep getting out of your chair to use the trash can or have stray shavings smudging your drawing.

INTERESTING FACT → The cardinal bird was named after the cardinals of the Roman Catholic Church and their bright red robes and caps.

More Funky Things to Draw—Birds

SWAN ⭐ ⭐

Swans are majestic waterfowl that have long, elegant necks and the ability to glide effortlessly on water. Young swan chicks, called cygnets, swim easily, but they are sometimes carried on the backs of adults as they swim. Swans have short legs, so they use the water as a runway, pattering across the surface before propelling themselves into the air. Swans can be very territorial and will attack people who enter their habitat.

Before You Begin

Observe that the swan is made up of a series of irregular shapes. The shapes for the wing and body look like leaves. For each step, study the changes between the soft line work and the shading of the feathers.

Step 1

Lightly draw the circle for the head. Sketch the neck curving down from behind the circle, and add the beak. Next, connect a leaf-shaped body to the neck, drawing a curved line around the middle for the water. From the base of the neck, draw a leaf-shaped wing pointing outward.

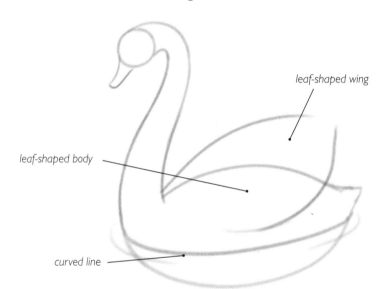

leaf-shaped wing

leaf-shaped body

curved line

Step 2

Draw the pointy back part of the beak. Then add the nostril and eye. Form the pointy outline of the wing and tail area. Add a curved line pattern to the tail. Define and darken the outline of the whole swan. Erase any lines you no longer need.

pointy back of beak

pointy feathers

bumpy feathers

cygnet

curved water lines

cygnet

Step 3

Study the bumpy pattern over the wing and neck area. Working down from the top of the wing, softly draw bumpy line work for the feathers then add the details on the neck. When drawing the cygnets, start with the head and beak, and then add the body. Draw faint, curved lines for water.

Step 4

With light pencil pressure, gradually build up a medium level of tone for the head and neck area. Softly make the marks going up the swan's back. Observe how there is no shading in some areas to make the feathers look shiny. Work around the tail and wing, darkening the shading where it's needed. Next, shade the details on your cygnets. Once you add the reflections in the water and the pond behind, your swan will be ready to glide!

DRAWING TIP

When trying to create light shading, pretend your pencil is a feather. This will remind you to hold it lightly.

INTERESTING FACT → Swans mate for life. The male and female have a strong bond and participate in building the nest and caring for the young.

More Funky Things to Draw—Birds

FLAMINGO ⭐ ⭐

Flamingos are striking birds with colorful plumage and long necks and legs. They can be found in tropical environments, living in salt lagoons and volcanic lakes. Flamingos skim shrimp and blue-green algae from the surface of the water with their unusual beaks. The bacteria they consume during this process are full of carotenoids, which provide flamingos with their distinctive bright pink or red coat of feathers. Flamingo courtship rituals look like synchronized dances.

Before You Begin

The flamingo is made up of a series of construction lines, joints, and curved shapes. The flamingo's body and the leg that it stands on are the most important elements of this picture. Also observe the neck shape and how it curves its way down from the right side of the body toward the baseline.

Step 1

Lightly draw the body shape at an angle. Draw the neck shape curving down from the right side of the body. Add an oval for the head and the beak shape. Next, sketch the straight leg, bending it slightly at the knee joint. Sketch the baseline under the leg. Make sure the beak isn't touching it. Finally, sketch the flamingo's right leg, bending it sharply at the knee joint. Add the foot shape next to the knee joint of the left leg.

Step 2

Draw the tail shape on the left corner of the body. Define and smooth the outline of the flamingo's body, neck, and head. Form the shapes of the legs around the joints and construction lines. Sketch the curvy shape of the wing at an angle.

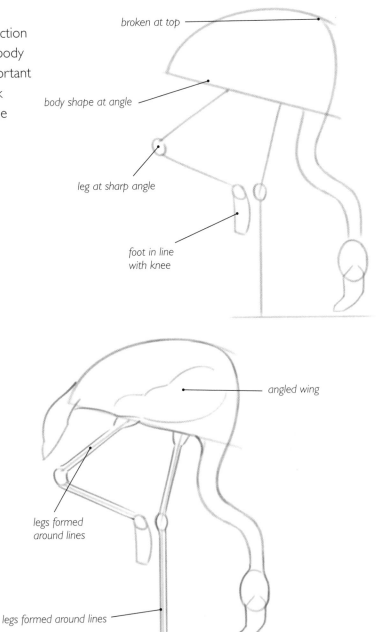

broken at top

body shape at angle

leg at sharp angle

foot in line with knee

angled wing

legs formed around lines

legs formed around lines

Step 3

Observe all the added details. Smooth and darken the flamingo's outline. Draw the eye at the top of the beak and the lines inside the beak. Draw the lines for the toes. Sketch the soft feathery lines for the wing, body, and tail. Draw the pointed tail feathers inside the tail shape.

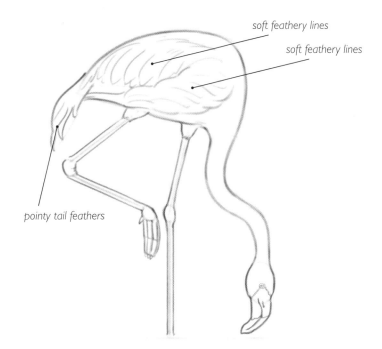

soft feathery lines

soft feathery lines

pointy tail feathers

DRAWING TIP

Don't be afraid to experiment by adding other shading to your drawing with colored pencils.

Step 4

Farther darken and define the outline of the flamingo. Using light pencil pressure, build up the shading on the underside of the body and the feathers to create highlights. Gently add tone around the neck, head, and beak. Draw fine lines across the legs from top to bottom. Sketch soft lines for water reflections. Once you have added rocks in the background, your flamingo is ready to take a drink!

INTERESTING FACT → Flamingos are often found standing on one leg, even when they are asleep!

SULFUR-CRESTED COCKATOO

The cockatoo is a popular and iconic Australian bird that belongs to the parrot family. This large white bird has a yellow crest and can be recognized by the noisy screeching sounds it makes. Throughout the continent, it can be found mainly in rural habitats and around human settlements. Cockatoos feed on berries, seeds, and nuts, and are happy to take food from people.

Before You Begin

Pay close attention to how the whole body of the cockatoo is at an angle over the branch. The shapes the cockatoo is built around appear to stack up on top of each other. Note also how the crest shape curves over to the left.

Step 1

Lightly sketch the branch. For the body, draw an egg shape on an angle above it. Sit an angled oval on top and slightly to the left of the egg for the head. Draw a fan shape for the tail. Sketch the v-shape that is inside the tail. Add the curved, pointed shape of the crest to the head, drawing a line inside. Next, thicken the neck by connecting the head and body area with lines.

Step 2

Starting at the front of the crest, draw the line across that separates the first feather. Sketch the other five wavy feathers inside the crest shape. Draw the sharp beak below the crest. Add the eye just above and in from the beak. Sketch the parallel leg shapes on either side of the body, and then draw the feet over the branch. Beginning at the top of the body, draw curved wings around the body and legs.

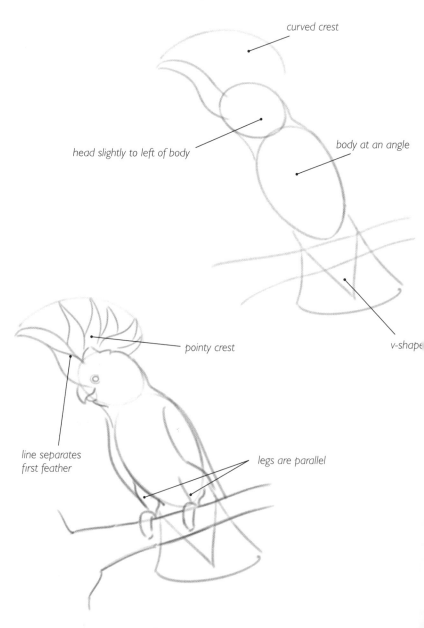

curved crest

head slightly to left of body

body at an angle

v-shape

pointy crest

line separates first feather

legs are parallel

Step 3

Define the jagged outline for feathers of the crest, head and wings. Starting on the left side of the tail, use lines to create the fan pattern inside the tail. Draw the claws for the feet, adding the fine lines across.

jagged line for feathers

jagged line for feathers

pattern on claws

Step 4

Using light pencil pressure, shade highlights inside the crest. Work your way down the cockatoo's body to build up the different levels of shading. Note how it is darker around certain parts of the body. Once you add the bark pattern on the tree and draw the leaves in the background, your cockatoo is ready to talk!

DRAWING TIP

If you always draw lightly at first, you have a better chance of erasing your mistakes!

INTERESTING FACT → Cockatoos can be kept as pets, as they are usually friendly toward people. They can also be taught to speak!

More Funky Things to Draw—Birds

OSTRICH ★ ★ ★

People have hunted ostriches for thousands of years for their meat and their prized plumage. Ostriches are the largest living land bird in the world, standing at over eight feet tall, and they lay the largest eggs. Ostriches are able to hide from enemies by crouching on the ground, where their coloring makes them almost invisible, or they can run away at over 40 miles an hour. Ostriches have a wicked kick, which allows them to defend themselves against lions.

Before You Begin

Observe how the ostrich is built around a series of shapes, construction lines, and joints. Also, study the changes in each step for how the feathers are drawn. Pay attention to the different types of line work that create the different levels of fine and large feathers. Be careful to follow the order of instructions for each step.

Step 1

Always draw lightly at first. Sketch a pebble-shaped body and draw the neck shape curving up from the right side. At the top, add the round head and beak shape. For the front leg, draw an oval for the hip joint, adding a bent line for the leg. Draw a bent line for the back leg. Next, add knee, ankle and foot joints to both legs. Sketch the baseline below the feet, so the ostrich looks like it is floating.

Step 2

Build the legs around the construction lines and joints. Lightly draw wavy outlines for the wing and tail shapes. Pay attention to the wavy pencil line of the feathers under the body. Add marks for feathers around the body and shapes on the back of the feet. Draw pointy toes on the feet.

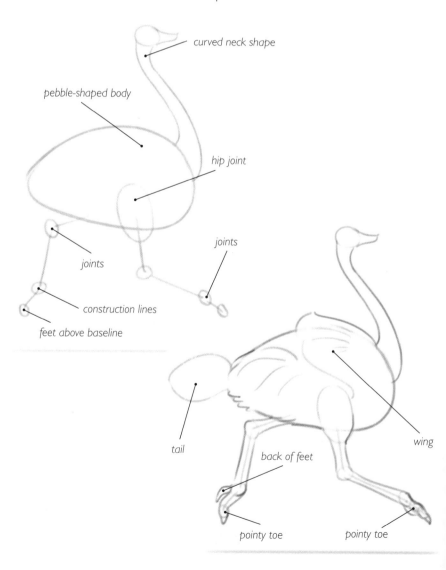

curved neck shape

pebble-shaped body

hip joint

joints

joints

construction lines

feet above baseline

tail

back of feet

wing

pointy toe

pointy toe

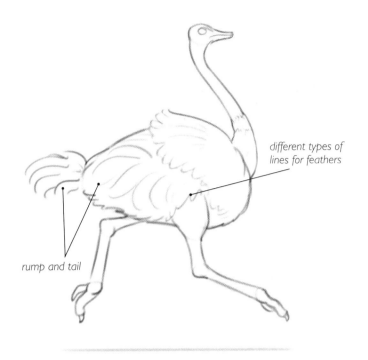

different types of lines for feathers

rump and tail

Step 3

Observe the different types of lines that have been drawn for feathers. Draw faint marks for feathers around the neck. Sketch a bumpy outline for the wing that extends around to the chest. Develop curved line work for feathers on the rump and tail. Next, add the eye and a line inside the beak.

Step 4

Observe the different levels of shading over the ostrich's form and the fine marks that add more feathers. Using light pencil pressure, work your way down from head to tail, drawing all the soft lines for feathers that you see. With medium pencil pressure, shade all the darker levels of tone from head to toe. Farther define the legs with fine marks. Finally, draw a shadow, wavy grass, and the background, and your ostrich is ready to run!

DRAWING TIP

Drawing skills develop with practice and experience. If you follow each instruction carefully and in order, your skills will improve over time.

INTERESTING FACT → During mating season, the male ostrich makes loud booming calls and puts on elaborate displays.

EURASIAN KINGFISHER

The kingfisher is found in parts of North Africa, Europe, and Asia. It mainly inhabits aquatic environments such as freshwater streams and rivers. The presence of a kingfisher indicates a healthy ecosystem. They are small and swift birds that feed on fish by diving into water. Kingfishers have vividly colored plumage that is greenish blue on the crown, back, and wings. The rump and tail are cobalt blue and the underside is a rich cinnamon color.

Before You Begin

The kingfisher's form is constructed using a series of oval and triangular shapes. To draw the kingfisher, you must position the shapes on the correct angles, using the baseline as your guide. Also, pay attention to how the kingfisher's outline is contoured around the shapes. Feathers can be tricky to draw, so for each step, study the various types of line drawn for feathers and the different levels of shading.

Step 1

With light pencil pressure, draw a baseline. Sketch an oval for the body at an angle above the end of the baseline. On top of the body, draw an oval for the head and sketch pointed shapes for the open beak. Add a triangular tail under the body, dropping it below the baseline. Square off the back of the head with straight lines. Sketch the leg shapes under the body, putting the feet on the baseline.

Step 2

Smooth and define the curves of the kingfisher's outline, especially around the tail and leg area. Draw a circle for the eye, adding line work around it. Sketch wavy lines for the wing and tail feathers. Draw a small line inside the beak.

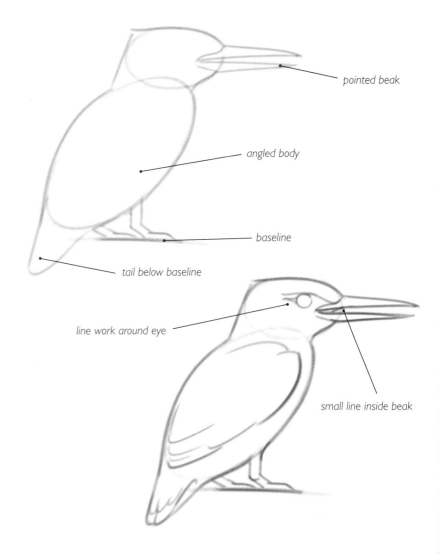

pointed beak

angled body

baseline

tail below baseline

line work around eye

small line inside beak

Step 3

Darken the kingfisher's outline. Using light pencil pressure, begin drawing soft lines across the head area. Next, draw a wavy pattern for feathers from the top of the wing, working down to the tail. Don't forget the feathery marks around the top of the leg, and the fish overlapping the beak. From the baseline, draw an uneven rectangular shape for the stump.

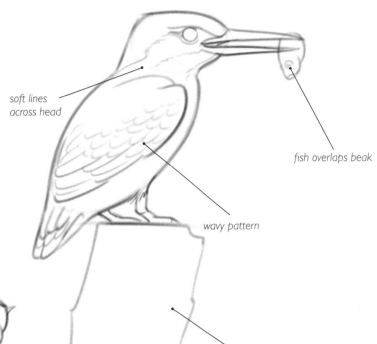

soft lines across head

fish overlaps beak

wavy pattern

uneven shape

Step 4

Study the different levels of shading and detail over the kingfisher's form. Using light pencil pressure, begin creating the softer levels of tone from head to toe. Define the fish. With medium pencil pressure, shade darker levels of tone around the bird's eye, beak, wing, and belly. Note the feathery lines added under the belly. Next, darken the pupil of the eye, leaving a dot of white. Draw the line work for the texture of the bark. Once you sketch the river in the background, your kingfisher will be ready to swallow the fish!

DRAWING TIP

Eyes aren't always easy to draw, especially when they are realistic. It's a good idea to practice drawing them by creating a page of experiments.

INTERESTING FACT

→ Kingfishers are very territorial and control the waterways where they feed. They need to do this as they must eat 60 percent of their body weight each day to survive.

PEACOCK ★ ★ ★

Peacock is a common name given to a species of bird from the pheasant family. Technically, the male bird is a peacock and the female is a peahen. Together they are peafowls. The male is one of the most stunning animals in the world, boasting dramatic tail feathers. The peacock's distinctive train makes up 60 percent of its body length. When it fans its tail plumage outward and displays its "eye" markings, it reveals an array of brilliant colors that include blue, green, gold, and red.

Before You Begin

The peacock is a complex bird to draw because of the angle of its body and its many layers of fine feathers. In the third step, pay attention to how the feathers fan off from the centerpiece of the tail. Note also how the "eye" markings travel around the tail in an even half-circle pattern. Take your time, study each step, follow the instructions carefully, and always draw lightly at first.

Step 1

Sketch a baseline at an angle and add a round body shape a small distance above it. Draw leg shapes under the body with the feet sitting over the baseline. Sketch the head, neck, and beak facing to your left. Now draw the angled half-circle for the tail fan from one side of the baseline to the other.

Step 2

Starting from the left side of the drawing, sketch the border of the tail fan, draping it over the body and onto the baseline. Draw the tail centerpiece curving around from the neck to the border. Add the eye and the crest to the peacock's head. Define and darken the outline of the whole body.

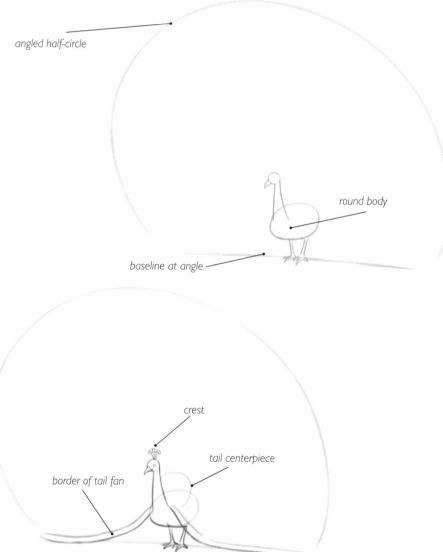

angled half-circle

round body

baseline at angle

crest

tail centerpiece

border of tail fan

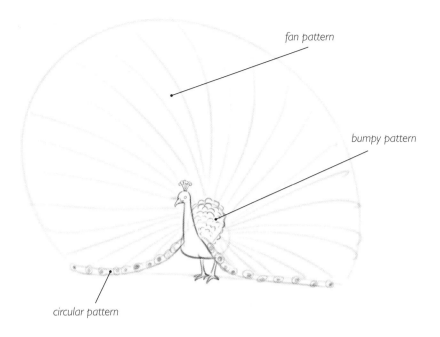

fan pattern

bumpy pattern

circular pattern

Step 3

Decorate the border with a circular pattern. Draw bumpy marks inside the tail centerpiece to represent feathers. Starting on the left side of the illustration, sketch the line pattern for feathers, fanning out inside the tail.

Step 4

Draw eye markings around the tail centerpiece in a half-circle pattern, from the edge outward. Continue to repeat the pattern in the same direction until you reach the top of the tail. From the centerpiece, begin adding soft pencil marks for the fine feathers. Note how they are lighter at the top. With medium pencil pressure, shade a darker level of tone around the peacock's body. Once you add a shadow underneath, your peacock will be ready to show off!

DRAWING TIP

To avoid smudging your picture with your hand or arm, try turning the page around as you draw!

INTERESTING FACT → A peacock's brilliant plumage reflects a range of colors. This is called the "Bragg reflection."

More Funky Things to Draw

Flowers

Paul Könye ✿ **Kate Ashforth**

Flowers

More Funky Things to Draw

Flowers

INTRODUCTION

The sight of a garden full of colorful flowers against a bright blue sky is enough to make anyone feel happy. People and flowers have had a love affair for thousands of years. Different varieties captivate our senses, heal particular ailments, and act as symbols for different feelings. Certain flowers have inspired people to create great works of art, poetry, and literature. When arranged in a vase, flowers bring a dash of color to a room, and flower essences can be mixed together to create perfume. In cultures around the world, flowers play a significant part in marking special occasions, as offerings in religious ceremonies, and to show someone you love them!

THINGS YOU WILL NEED

- A gray lead pencil (HB or 2B).
- A pencil sharpener and a dish for shavings.
- Sheets of drawing paper.
- A clean eraser.
- Patience—learning drawing skills takes time and practice.
- Confidence—a positive attitude will help to develop your drawing skills!

Drawing Guidelines

1 There is a process in learning to draw. Follow the steps carefully and in order.
2 Always use light pencil pressure when beginning the first stage of a drawing.
3 If you feel unsure about the instructions, ask an adult for help.
4 Gray lead smudges easily. Pay attention to where your hand is on the page.
5 Clean the gray lead residue off your eraser by rubbing it against a spare piece of paper.

Beginner   Intermediate   Expert

The stars at the top of each page grade the difficulty level of each drawing from beginner to intermediate or expert. Some drawings are trickier than others because of the level of detail, but if you carefully follow the basic principles of building a drawing from shapes and lines, you will learn to conquer both simple and complex drawings.

Follow the Steps

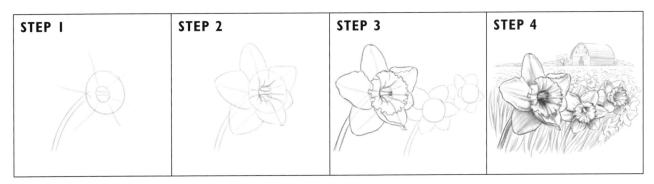

| STEP 1 | STEP 2 | STEP 3 | STEP 4 |

Study the changes between each step and the pencil techniques used. You will notice that flowers are drawn using a series of rounded and pointed shapes and different types of line. Shading helps to define the petals and leaves.

PENCIL TECHNIQUES

The boxes below show three types of pencil work drawn for pattern.

| soft pattern | defined pattern | fine pattern |

Observe the types of marks or lines that are drawn for patterns on each flower's petals or leaves. Are they fine or soft? Are they short marks or longer lines? The patterns are repeated and are drawn using a change in pencil pressure.

The lines, shapes, and patterns that make up the construction of a flower require lots of attention to detail. Follow one step at a time, drawing lightly as you go so you can erase any details you are unhappy with. It is vital that you get the first step drawn correctly so you can form the shape of your flower and achieve the right perspective.

Shading and Pencil Pressure

Shading adds detail and definition to a subject. Apply different levels of shading with changes in pencil pressure—a light pencil grip creates a light gray tone, for example.

The boxes below show different levels of gray tone created by a pencil.

Light   Medium   Dark

More Funky Things to Draw—Flowers

SUNFLOWERS ⭐⭐

Sunflowers are native to the Americas, most likely originating from Mexico. Sunflowers have dark cente
surrounded by sunny yellow petals. They also have hairy leaves. They stand straight and tall with some
varieties growing up to 15 feet in height! Early in history, Native Americans grew sunflowers for food
and medicine. Explorers brought the sunflower to Europe, where they were only considered to be a
decorative plant. They were also exported to Russia, Spain, and China, where they are cultivated for o

Before You Begin

The sunflower drawing is based around a series of circles. You will observe that the larger circle is tilted (looking up) and the smaller circles inside are positioned near the top. It is important that you draw these elements correctly so you achieve the right perspective. Also pay attention to how the petals are layered between the steps.

Step 1

Lightly draw a large, slightly tilted circle for the flower head. Sketch two smaller circles inside, a little off-center. The head of the flower should appear to be looking upward. Draw the stem coming down from the center.

Step 2

Observe how some of the petals are layered. Starting at your left, draw the petal next to the stem. Going clockwise, draw the larger, pointed petals around the center, and then sketch the smaller ones poking out from underneath. Add a curved line to the middle of the flower.

smaller circles off-center

line inside

tilted circle

smaller petals underneath

start with petal next to stem

fine marks

darker in center

fuzzy outline

faint dot pattern

Step 3

Draw a fuzzy outline around each circle. With light pencil pressure, sketch fine marks inside the middle circle and around the outside. Note how it is a darker tone in the middle. Draw a faint dot pattern around the edge of the center circle. Starting under the flower head, draw leaves poking out from the stem.

DRAWING TIP

Before you begin a drawing, study the different levels of gray tone that you see in the final step. Are they light, medium, or dark?

Step 4

Define the leaf shapes and add the light pattern inside. With light pencil pressure, shade light gray tone around the petals and leaves. Shade medium tone around the center of the flower and on the petals behind. Define the flower's center and shade a darker tone behind the petals and on the stem. Once you add smaller sunflowers in the background, your sunflower will reach toward the sun!

INTERESTING FACT → Sunflower seeds are a popular snack around the world.

More Funky Things to Draw—Flowers

ORIENTAL LILY

Oriental lilies descended from a species native to Japan and Korea and have flourished in gardens for more than 3,000 years. They are related to asparagus, lily-of-the-valley, and hyacinth flowers. Orient are highly popular flowers, often chosen for arrangements because of their heady fragrance. Their scer has been used in the making of perfume throughout history. Oriental lilies are often used to represent purity, innocence, and beauty, and are frequently chosen as wedding flowers.

Before You Begin

A circle is used to construct the form of the Oriental lily. A smaller circle with construction lines is drawn in the center to help guide you in positioning the petals, which fan out to the edges of the larger circle. It is important that you pay attention to the angle of the stem and layering of the petals and leaves to achieve the correct perspective.

Step 1

Lightly draw a large circle with a small circle in the center. Draw an angled stem that points to the small circle. Sketch the construction lines fanning out around the center circle: four on top of the circle and two at the bottom.

Step 2

Observe that all petals are drawn around construction lines and curve over on the ends. Draw the top petal first, from the center up to the edge of the circle. Follow the same process by drawing the large petal to your right. Moving clockwise, sketch the next two petals. Draw the layered petal poking out from behind the top petal. Finally, draw the small petal on the right, behind the others.

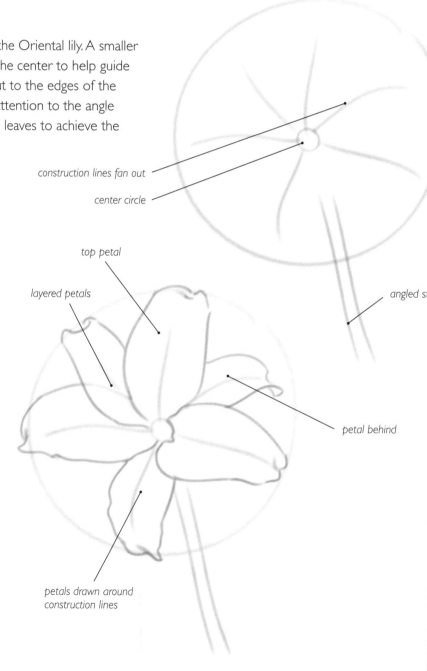

construction lines fan out

center circle

top petal

layered petals

angled st

petal behind

petals drawn around
construction lines

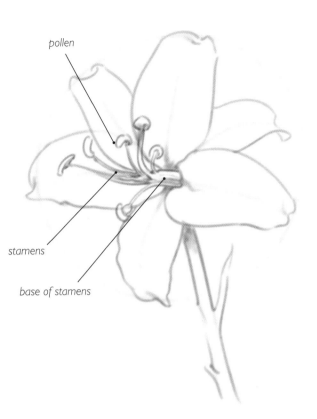

pollen

stamens

base of stamens

Step 3

Draw a base for the stamens coming out from the center and pointing to your left. Sketch the stamens at different lengths, fanning out from the base, and add the pollen. Define and darken the outline of the petals and create the outline of the stem.

DRAWING TIP

When you are drawing a gray lead picture, place a piece of paper over sections you've already drawn so you don't smudge them.

Step 4

Define and darken the center of the lily first and then concentrate on the stamens. Using light pencil pressure, shade the detail in the middle of the petals and add the dot pattern over the top. For the stem, draw the four leaves in front fanning outward and then add the four leaves behind. Lightly draw the soft line pattern on the leaves. Once you shade the gray tone over the leaves and stem, your lily will be ready to release a heavenly scent!

INTERESTING FACT → Oriental lily petals can be mixed with honey and used as an ointment to soften the skin. They are often put in "anti-aging" facial creams.

More Funky Things to Draw—Flowers

DAFFODIL ★ ★

Daffodils have been cultivated in gardens for thousands of years. The Latin name for daffodil flowers is "narcissus," which comes from the Greek word "narkissos." In Greek mythology, Narcissus was a young man who was captivated by his own reflection. Varieties of daffodil can be found throughout the Mediterranean, North Africa, Europe, and the Americas. Originally daffodil petals and trumpets were yellow, orange, or white, but in modern times they have also been cultivated in pink, red, and green.

Before You Begin

The daffodil is constructed around two circles with lines fanning out from the center. It is important to achieve the correct positioning of circles, lines, and stem to draw the flower in the right perspective. Also, observe closely how the petals are larger on one side of the bloom and become smaller on the other, to make the main daffodil look like it is facing away to your right.

Step 1

Lightly draw the larger circle at a slight angle. Draw a smaller inner circle off-center. Fan construction lines for the petals out from the middle. Pay attention to the length of each line and the space between them. On your left, curve the stem up to the center of the bloom, drawing the pointed piece inside.

Step 2

To create the daffodil's trumpet, define the stamen and draw lines curving around the outside. Draw the largest petal around the construction line and then sketch the one above it. Now draw the smallest petal and sketch the ones on either side. Sketch the final petal underneath, making sure the petals overlap on either side.

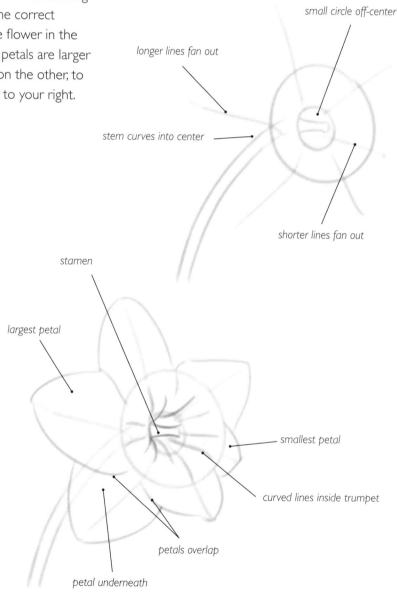

small circle off-center

longer lines fan out

stem curves into center

shorter lines fan out

stamen

largest petal

smallest petal

curved lines inside trumpet

petals overlap

petal underneath

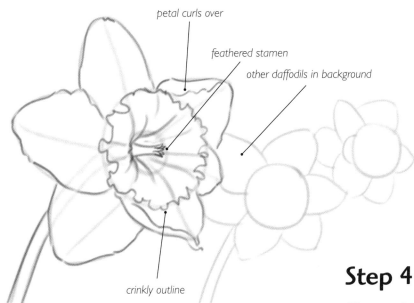

petal curls over

feathered stamen

other daffodils in background

crinkly outline

Step 3

Sketch a crinkly outline around the edge of the trumpet. Create the feathered tip of the stamen. Draw the curled edges of the two larger petals on your right. Define and darken the outlines of all the petals and the stem. Lightly draw other daffodil shapes in the background, paying attention to their positioning and size.

Step 4

Observe the light to dark levels of gray tone over the main daffodil. With light pencil pressure, shade the lines that fan out around the petals and trumpet. Build up the darker areas of tone around the petals, stem, and inner trumpet. Define the outlines of the petals and trumpets for all of the daffodils, and then add the shading. Draw the horizon line for the field in the background and sketch in the crop of daffodils. Once you add the barn and trees, your daffodils will sway in the breeze!

DRAWING TIP

The art term "horizon line" means the line that is drawn to separate the earth from the sky.

INTERESTING FACT → The Romans brought daffodils to Britain to cultivate because they believed that the sap had healing powers. However, crystals in the sap can actually irritate the skin.

More Funky Things to Draw—Flowers

IKEBANA ⭐⭐

In Japanese, "ikebana" means "living flowers." Ikebana is a traditional form of flower arranging that creates harmony and rhythm in linear construction and the use of color. The Japanese emphasize the simplicity and elegance of the flowers. The ikebana art form includes the careful arrangement of the stems, blooms, leaves, branches, and vase. The construction process is based around three main points that symbolize heaven, Earth, and humankind.

Before You Begin

The ikebana arrangement is based around a series of shapes. The tabletop and block-shaped vase support the arrangement. The rest of the ikebana is structured around two straight bamboo sticks that stand up from the center of the vase. Focusing on this in the drawing process will help you draw the arrangement from the right perspective.

Step 1

Lightly draw an ellipse (a flattened oval) for the table and add two small lines under the tabletop. Draw the block shape coming up from the center of the ellipse. Notice how the sides of the block angle in. Sketch the curved rectangular shape over the top with a rectangle in the center and add two sticks above. Draw the side of the vase with two fine lines. Add two lines curving over the sticks for the flower stems.

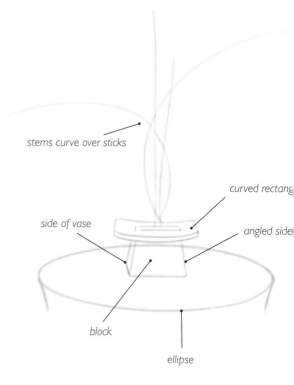

stems curve over sticks

side of vase

curved rectang

angled side

block

ellipse

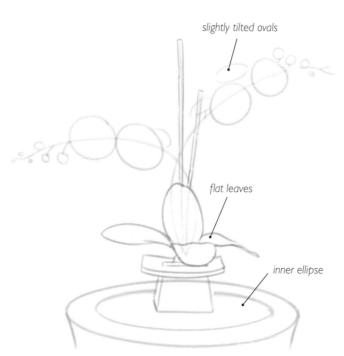

slightly tilted ovals

flat leaves

inner ellipse

Step 2

Draw a smaller off-center ellipse inside the tabletop. Draw the middle, bottom leaf that is like a half circle. Sketch an oval leaf over the sticks and draw two flat leaves either side. Draw slightly tilted ovals around the stems and add the small buds at the ends.

Step 3

Shape the petals of the main flowers inside the ovals and define the buds and the smaller flowers in the background. Add the details to the centers of all flowers and define the sticks and stems. Using a light pencil grip, shade the pattern over the leaves. Add the shadows over the vase and tabletop and any further details over the arrangement. Now your ikebana is ready to reach for the heavens!

INTERESTING FACT → The art form of ikebana began as a ritual offering made at Buddhist temples. Later it became an important part of women's schooling in preparation for marriage.

More Funky Things to Draw—Flowers

ROSE ★ ★ ★

Roses have been mentioned in many ancient tales since their cultivation began in Asia about 5,000 years ago. They are often used as confetti for celebrations, for medicinal purposes, and of course for bathing and perfume. Roses were in such high demand during the 17th century that rose water could be used like money. Since the 19th century roses have become available in a range of colors like white, pink, red, yellow, orange, mauve, and green.

Before You Begin

Roses are difficult to draw because of the many layers of irregular petals. You will notice that the petals spiral out from the center of each bloom. Carefully study all the steps to observe the different shapes for each petal, and how the petals fan outward and are connected to one another. Also, observe closely the levels of shading in step 4 that give the roses definition.

Step 1

Lightly draw a circle for the rose on your left. Sketch an irregular shape with a curved and pointed outline for the rose below. Above, draw the rosebud on your right with a stem. Sketch the smaller rosebud in the middle and add spirals to the three open roses.

Step 2

For this step, study how the petals have been drawn on top of the spirals. Observe how the petals fan out from the center of the spiral. For the rosebud on your right, draw the center first and then slowly connect each petal. Do the same for the rose below and the one on your left. Draw the crinkled edges of the rosebud in the middle.

spiral

pointed

spiral

circle

curved

spiral

irregular shape

petals fan out from center

petals on top of spiral

curved lines

small leaves

pointed outline

crinkled outline

Step 3

For all roses, draw one petal at a time. Slowly draw the crinkled outline of each petal for the rose on your left. For the rose below, draw the curved and pointed outline of each petal. For the rosebud on your right, sketch curved lines that wrap around the center. Complete the rosebud in the middle and define the stems with small leaves.

Step 4

Study the different levels of gray tone that are shaded on each petal. Beginning at the outer edges of each rose, use light pencil pressure to softly shade the lighter gray tone around the edges of the petals. With medium pencil pressure, build up the darker levels of tone that create the shadows around the petals. Add the crinkled leaf shapes to the stems. Once you add the fine patterns inside the leaves, you will be ready to smell the roses!

DRAWING TIP

Practice drawing the layers of petals over a spiral before you start your final drawing.

INTERESTING FACT → The rose is around 35 million years old and there are over 30,000 known varieties.

More Funky Things to Draw—Flowers

ORCHID ★ ★ ★

Orchids have uniquely shaped petals and long-lasting, delicate blooms. There are an estimated 25,000 species of orchids around the world, with more still being discovered and bred. Orchids have long been used as a remedy for illness and an ingredient in love potions. They are considered a symbol of beauty, wealth, and love. A vanilla bean is actually the stamen of a Mexican Vanilla planifolia orchid, and is the source of vanilla flavoring.

Before You Begin

Observe how the orchid flowers are constructed over a cross. This is used as a guide so you can position the bow-shaped petals over the top. Study how the orchid flowers are drawn at a slight angle and how they are spaced apart. Also, pay attention to how the petals are layered and the fine details that are drawn in the center of each flower.

Step 1

With light pencil pressure, draw the tilted cross at the top. Follow with two crosses underneath that stagger down your page. Pay attention to their angles. Draw bow-shaped petals over the crosses, making sure they are centered.

Step 2

For the top bloom, draw a column under the center of the flower, following the downstroke of the cross. Add the orchid's lip, again lining it up over the cross. Repeat this process with the other two blooms. With light pencil pressure, add shading to all blooms.

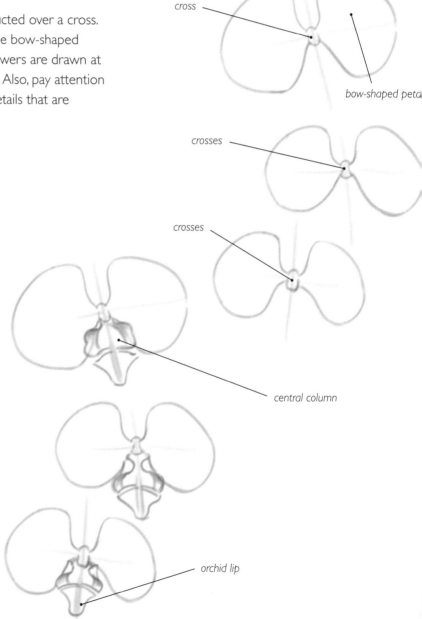

cross

bow-shaped peta

crosses

crosses

central column

orchid lip

Step 3

Define the wobbly edges of each orchid's outline. Lightly draw the triangular petals behind the bow-shaped petals. Define the stamen in the center of each bloom and add the fine details around it. Define the lip, adding a thin line around the outside.

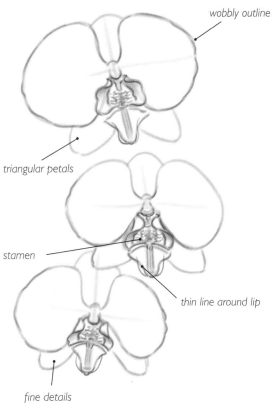

wobbly outline

triangular petals

stamen

thin line around lip

fine details

Step 4

Using light pencil pressure, sketch the soft lines running across the petals of each bloom and shade the light levels of gray tone over the orchid. With a medium pencil grip, shade the medium levels of tone around the middle of each bloom, and then define and darken the details. In the background, softly draw the stem of the orchid curving behind the flowers in the foreground. Once you add the other blooms and buds, your orchid will be ready to flourish!

DRAWING TIP

The foreground is the area in focus in the front of the picture. The background is the area behind or around the foreground.

INTERESTING FACT → Orchids are commonly thought of as a tropical flower, but they actually grow almost everywhere except glaciers and deserts.

More Funky Things to Draw—Flowers

TULIP ⭐⭐

Tulips originated in Central Asia. Travelers brought tulip bulbs back to Turkey about 1,000 years ago. In the 16th century, they spread to the Netherlands, where high prices were charged for bulbs because of their popularity. This period was dubbed "tulipmania" and farmers began speculating in the tulip trade. Single bulbs were priced as high as $1,000. The Dutch continue to grow their favorite flower and they remain the chief source of tulips in the world.

Before You Begin

The tulip flower itself is fairly easy to draw. The most important elements to consider when drawing a tulip are how the petals and leaves fold around one another. The most difficult aspect of this picture is the background. Observe closely how the flowers behind are constructed using a V-shaped formation. This acts as a guide to help you draw the tulips in perspective.

Step 1

Lightly draw a curved stem with a bump at the base. At the top, draw two petals opening outward. Draw a curve between the tops of the petals.

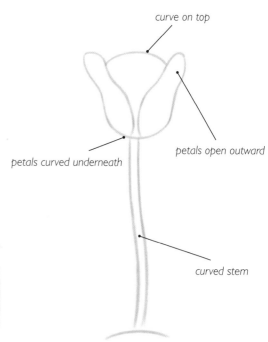

curve on top

petals curved underneath

petals open outward

curved stem

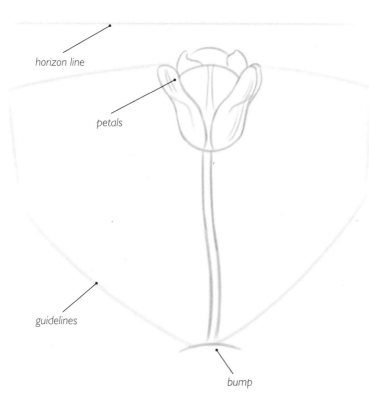

horizon line

petals

guidelines

bump

Step 2

Using light pencil pressure, draw guidelines on eith- side of the bump. Form the open petals by adding curved lines inside the shapes. Add two lines in the middle of the tulip and smaller petals on top. Light draw a curved guideline behind the tulip and a horizon line above it.

tulips in perspective

tulips in back are smaller

Step 3

Starting at your left, draw leaf shapes coming up from the bump of the main tulip, wrapping them around the stem. On each side, draw the leaves for the tulips next in line and add their stems and petals. Remember to fit them between the guidelines for proper perspective.

DRAWING TIP

Form is an art element that describes the complete, three-dimensional shape of an object. Form can be created with shading or pattern.

Step 4

Define the petals of the tulips behind. Lightly draw the heads of the tulips in the background, drawing one row at a time. Make sure they get smaller and sit under the guideline. With medium pencil pressure, add medium levels of gray tone to the petals and leaves of all the tulips. Once you add shading for the ground and the windmill and trees on the horizon line, your tulips will be ready to sway in the breeze!

INTERESTING FACT ➡ The name tulip is derived from the Turkish word "tülbent," which means "turban."

More Funky Things to Draw—Flowers

BIRD OF PARADISE

Bird of paradise flowers originate in South Africa. The unusual, colorful flower has a green "beak" and a bright orange and blue "crest," and silvery, waxy green leaves that fan out from the stem. Sunbirds perch on the sturdy bloom to pollinate the flowers. As they feast on the nectar, the flower opens up, covering their feet in pollen. Bird of paradise flowers are admired for their dramatic appearance and their beautiful lines of structure and emphasis.

Before You Begin

The flower is made up of a series of pointed shapes. It is important to study each step to understand how the pointed shapes connect to the stem and overlap one another. Also, pay close attention to the shapes of the petals. Look at each one's sizes and curved outline, and its length and width.

Step 1

Lightly draw a tall stem that is pointed at the top. Add a sharp beak shape pointing to your right. Draw a shorter stem on an angle at the base of the tall stem. Add another sharp beak shape at the top that overlaps the tall stem in the middle.

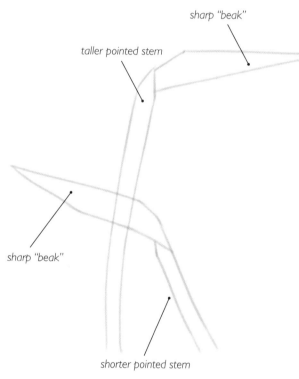

sharp "beak"

taller pointed stem

sharp "beak"

shorter pointed stem

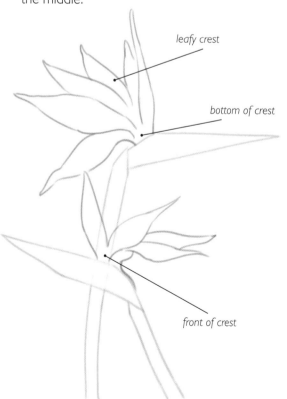

leafy crest

bottom of crest

front of crest

Step 2

Observe how the leaf-shaped flowers of the crest fan out from the tops of the flowers and overlap. For the tall stem, start at the bottom of the crest, drawing one petal at a time. For the short stem, start at the front, drawing one petal at a time.

smaller petals

smaller petals

Step 3

Define the details of the stems and beak shapes. For the tall flower, work your way around the crest, adding the smaller petals. For the smaller flower, start at the front of the flower and add the smaller petals around the crest.

DRAWING TIP

Look up pictures of these flowers to see what color they are. Then color your picture with colored pencils.

Step 4

Starting at your left, lightly draw leaf shapes fanning around the bottom of the flower stems. Draw faint lines for leaf patterns. With light pencil pressure, shade light gray tone around the stems, working your way up to the petals. Build up a darker level of tone to create shadowing around the base of the petals and down the tall stem. Once you add soft shading over the leaves, your bird of paradise will be ready to crane its head to the sun!

INTERESTING FACT → The bird of paradise is also known as the crane flower, and is related to the banana tree!

More Funky Things to Draw—Flowers

CHERRY BLOSSOM

Japan is famous for its white and pink ornamental cherry blossoms, called sakura. These flowers are a symbol of Japan and can be found in temples, shrines, and formal gardens as well as along city streets. There are 400 types of cherry trees in Japan but none of them bear fruit. During cherry blossom season people enjoy a tradition called hanami, going to observe and celebrate the beauty of the trees in bloom. Cherry blossoms are often depicted on Japanese ceramics, clothes, and paper.

Before You Begin

The drawing of the cherry blossoms is based around a branch and a series of circles, some of which are tilted or layered. It is important that you observe where the circles sit against or near the branch. Also, pay attention to the size of each circle and its angle.

Step 1

Lightly draw a forked branch with one crooked arm. Starting at the base of the branch, draw a large circle near the fork with a smaller circle inside. Continue drawing the rest of the circles up the branch, paying attention to their relative sizes and how they are layered or tilted.

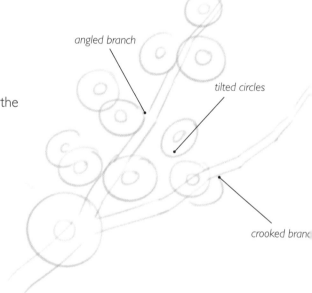

angled branch

tilted circles

crooked branch

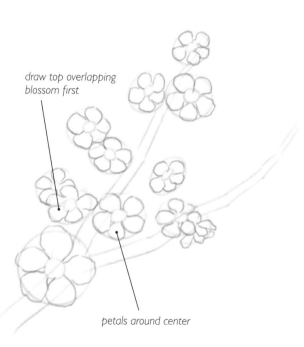

draw top overlapping blossom first

petals around center

Step 2

Starting at the base of the branch, draw petals inside each circle. Continue up the branch. Where blossoms overlap, draw the top one first.

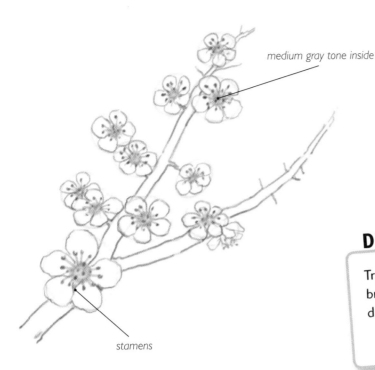

medium gray tone inside

stamens

Step 3

Define and darken the crooked branch, adding little spikes around the outline. With light pencil pressure, shade a medium gray tone inside the center of each blossom. Draw stamens with dots on the ends.

DRAWING TIP

Try adding a tree trunk and other branches to test your new drawing skills!

Step 4

Using light pencil pressure, shade light gray tone around the edges of the petals. Shade medium gray tone on the underside of the branch. Darken and define the center of each blossom. Lightly draw the edge of the water and the top of the mountain in the background. Once you add the trees and temple, your cherry blossoms will begin to fall!

INTERESTING FACT → In 1912, Japan gave 3,000 trees to the United States as a symbol of their growing friendship.

More Funky Things to Draw—Flowers

WARATAH ★ ★

Waratah is an Eora Aboriginal name of a striking Australian flower. It is typically found in a vibrant crimson, but hybrid forms have now been grown in white and pink. Waratah flowers have the unusual ability to survive bushfire season. After a fire, they regenerate from their roots and begin flowering two years later. The four species of waratah grow in the Australian states of New South Wales, Victoria, and Tasmania. The one shown here is a New South Wales waratah.

Before You Begin

The most important elements are the shape of the bloom and the pattern of the pointy flowers that cover it. Observe how the waratah is constructed using a bun shape. Also, carefully study how the flowers are layered over the teardrop shapes that run around the bottom of the flowerhead.

Step 1

Lightly draw a bun shape for the flowerhead. Draw a straight stem coming down from the middle. Starting at your left, draw the large petals fanning around the base of the bun shape.

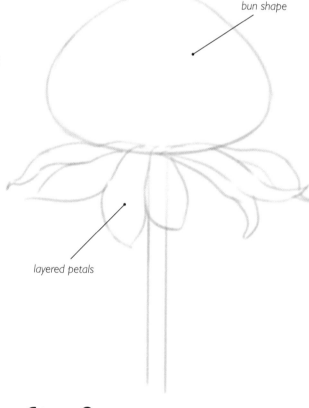

bun shape

layered petals

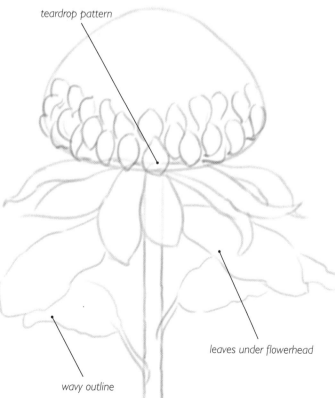

teardrop pattern

leaves under flowerhead

wavy outline

Step 2

Draw wavy leaves on either side of the stem. Sketch two smaller leaves underneath, sitting at the base of the stem. Starting at your right, draw a teardrop pattern for flowers around the base of the flowerhead. Layer the rest of the pattern above.

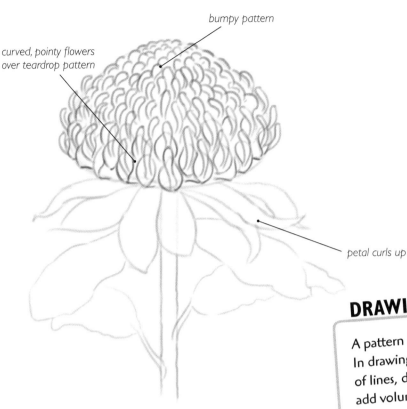

curved, pointy flowers over teardrop pattern

bumpy pattern

petal curls up

Step 3

Starting at the base of the flowerhead, draw curved, pointy flowers over the teardrop pattern one layer at a time. Continue to layer the flowers above until you complete the pattern. Then draw a bumpy pattern on top of the flowerhead. Define the petals, paying attention to how some curl up.

DRAWING TIP

A pattern is something that repeats. In drawing it could be a series of lines, dots, or shapes that add volume and definition to a subject.

Step 4

Create a spiky outline for the two large leaves and the smaller ones below. Lightly draw faint patterns inside. Define the stem and add the irregular pattern. Shade light gray tone around the edges of the leaves and petals. Build up darker levels of tone around the flowerhead and at the base of the flowers. Once you add the other shadows, your waratah will be ready to bloom!

INTERESTING FACT → Waratah are in the genus Telopea, which comes from the Greek word "telopos," meaning "seen from afar."

More Funky Things to Draw

Pony Club

Paul Könye • **Kate Ashforth**

More Funky Things to Draw

Pony Club

INTRODUCTION

Many children around the world dream of owning a horse or pony. Horses require feeding, grooming, and lots of space for regular exercise, but they repay this care with great affection and the fun of riding. Members of a pony club can learn riding skills and maneuvers for dressage. They might also prepare a horse for an event by grooming it and braiding its mane, and of course these talented riders wear neat and elegant riding clothes.

THINGS YOU WILL NEED

- A gray lead pencil (HB or 2B).
- A pencil sharpener and a dish for shavings.
- Sheets of drawing paper.
- A clean eraser.
- Patience—learning drawing skills takes time and practice.
- Confidence—a positive attitude will help to develop your drawing skills!

Drawing Guidelines

1 There is a process in learning to draw. Follow the steps carefully and in order.
2 Always use light pencil pressure when beginning the first stage of a drawing.
3 If you feel unsure about the instructions, ask an adult for help.
4 Gray lead smudges easily. Pay attention to where your hand is on the page.
5 Clean the gray lead residue off your eraser by rubbing it against a spare piece of paper.
6 Most of the directions for drawing people and animals don't mention the joints of the limbs or the hand and feet shapes, but they're still important! Be sure to draw them in.
7 In this chapter, many of the horses and ponies are light in color, so draw your guidelines lightly and erase them thoroughly once you no longer need them.

 Beginner   Intermediate   Expert

The stars at the top of each page grade the difficulty level of each drawing from beginner to intermediate or expert. Some drawings are trickier than others because of the level of detail, but if you carefully follow the basic principles of building a drawing from shapes and lines, you will learn to conquer both simple and complex drawings.

Follow the Steps

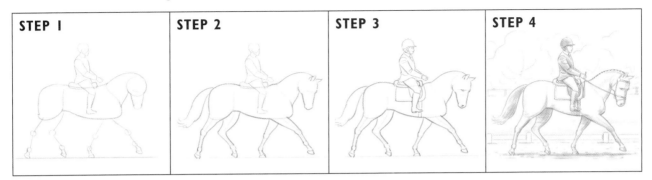

| STEP 1 | STEP 2 | STEP 3 | STEP 4 |

Start the drawing process by studying all aspects of the horse's body and pose. Carefully observe all the steps and see what is added in each one. Pay special attention to the positioning of the horse's neck and head. Baselines are often used to help you position legs on an angle. Observe the legs of the skeleton: their length and size, and whether they are bent or overlapping. Skeletons are also used to create the bodies of the children that appear throughout the following pages.

PENCIL TECHNIQUES FOR DRAWING A HORSE'S FORM

The boxes below show a variety of shapes that are drawn for a horse.

| 3D shapes | irregular shapes | shapes at an angle |

When you arrive at each page of this book, observe the types of shapes drawn for each subject. Are the shapes rounded or irregular? What size are they?

To draw a three-dimensional form, you must draw all shapes at the proper size and angle. Some parts of the horse may need to be drawn larger or smaller for proper perspective. Also, observe how the shapes are joined together. Leaving the paper white in places will add highlights to a horse, person, or object.

Shading and Pencil Pressure

Shading adds detail and definition to a subject. Apply different levels of shading with changes in pencil pressure—a light pencil grip creates a light gray tone, for example.

The boxes below show different levels of gray tone created by a change in pencil pressure.

Light Medium Dark

More Funky Things to Draw—Pony Club

DRESSAGE

Dressage (which rhymes with "massage") is a French word that means "training." Over hundreds of years, techniques for training horses evolved and in 1572 all dressage principles were officially established at the Imperial Riding School of Vienna, which was a center for equestrian excellence. In the 20th century, dressage grew into a popular competitive sport and now it even appears in the Olympics. To compete in dressage, you need a horse or pony that is capable of performing precise maneuvers.

Before You Begin

The dressage picture is made up of a series of irregular and rounded shapes. The legs of the horse are built using construction lines and joints. Pay close attention to the way the shapes are drawn for the rider's shoulders, chest, and arms.

Step 1

Lightly draw the rider's round head with a nose and jaw pointing to your right. Sketch the neck and back of the jacket and add the bent front arm. Now sketch the chest and back arm, making sure the hands connect. Sketch the horse's backbone and add a round head and curved neck. Draw the curved belly area and the rump. Sketch the rider's bent leg and saddle. Draw a baseline underneath the horse. Then sketch the front leg above the baseline and the other three against it.

Step 2

Starting at the horse's head, form its curved outline around the shapes, construction lines and joints. Draw its pointed ears and add a flowing tail to its rump that curves up on the end.

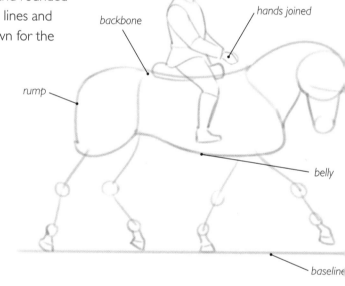

backbone

hands joined

rump

belly

baseline

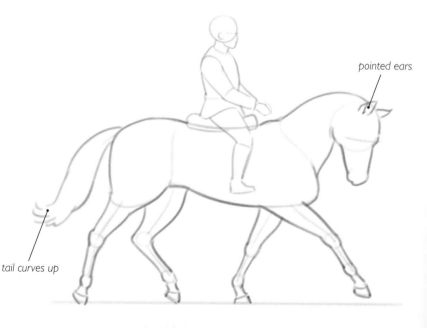

pointed ears

tail curves up

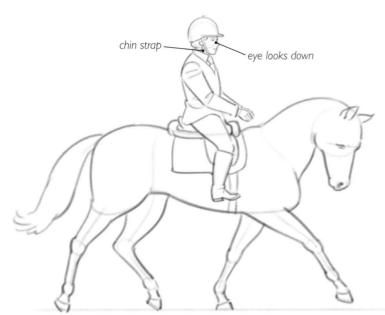

chin strap — eye looks down

Step 3

Form the rider's outline around the shapes. Add the helmet first and then develop the profile. Draw the hair and ear then add the strap under the chin. Work your way down the rider's body, drawing the details of riding apparel. Now add the saddle and girth.

Step 4

Study the different levels of shading over the whole picture. For the horse, draw the harness and add a dot pattern for the braided mane. With light pencil pressure, sketch the soft texture of the tail. Working your way down from the rider's helmet, shade light to medium gray tone over both figures. Focus on the darker tones of the saddle and the shadowing around the horse's legs. Once you draw the field in the background, your horse will be ready to jump!

DRAWING TIP

When you bake a cake, you should always read all the instructions first. Drawing is the same way! Study all the directions and drawings carefully before you start.

INTERESTING FACT → Some names of dressage moves are passage, piaffe, pirouette, half-pass, and flying changes.

More Funky Things to Draw—Pony Club

FEEDING A HORSE ⭐⭐

You have to be careful what you feed a horse because they have delicate stomachs. Horses are grazing animals that love to snack. The most natural food for a horse is good quality pasture or hay. Richer food like grain can also be given as a supplement to their diet, especially for active and pregnant horses. Horses need plenty of fresh water and the occasional salt mineral block to munch on.

Before You Begin

The drawing of the girl is based on a skeleton, and the horse is made up of a series of rounded shapes. The most important part of this drawing is the angle of the girl's head, spine, and hips. Also pay attention to the positioning of the horse's head and the bucket.

Step 1

For the girl, lightly draw a round head with a face cross and chin looking down to your left. Draw her angled spine. Sketch a rounded chest on an angle and a tilted oval for her hips. Draw the shorter back arm and then the bent front arm. Add her hand shapes and the bucket at an angle. Now add her legs. For the horse, draw an egg-shaped head with a muzzle overlapping the bucket. Add the horse's neck.

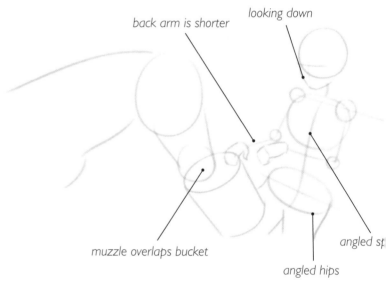

Step 2

Starting at the girl's neck, draw her curved outline around the skeleton. For the horse, draw the front upturned ear and floppy forelock (hair that drapes over the forehead). Add the back ear and shape the muzzle. Sketch bumpy shapes over the horse's spine and a curved line for the mane.

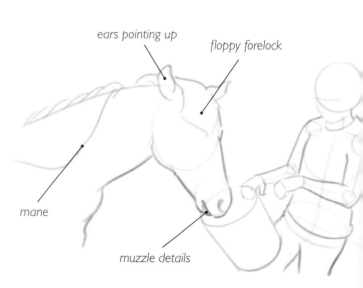

Step 3

Draw the girl's eyes, nose, and mouth over the cross. Draw a cowboy hat on her head and then shape her face and braided hair. Sketch a curved line for the bucket's handle behind her hands. Draw her fingers inside the hand shapes and add the details of her clothing and the bucket. Draw the horse's eye under its forelock. Darken and define their outlines.

curved bucket handle

Step 4

With light pencil pressure, create the texture of the horse's mane using soft lines. Draw the lines for the wall. Sketch the outline of the gate and add a diagonal crosshatch pattern. Sharpen your pencil and sketch the fine texture of the girl's hair. Working your way down both figures, add light to medium gray shading. Now your horse is ready to be fed!

DRAWING TIP

Find a place to draw that has good natural light. This will help you see the details of your artwork clearly.

INTERESTING FACT → Some treats that are safe to give horses are apples, raisins, sugar cubes, and sunflower seeds.

More Funky Things to Draw—Pony Club

GALLOPING

Every horse can walk, trot, canter, and gallop. These different types of movement are called gaits. Galloping is the fastest gait. The average gallop speed is around 30 miles an hour, and over short distances, a galloping American quarter horse can go almost twice that fast! A gallop makes a distincti one-two-three-four sound, and sometimes all four of the horse's hooves leave the ground at once. If you've ever watched a horse race, you've seen horses galloping.

Before You Begin

The drawing of the rider is built using a skeleton. The horse is constructed using rounded and irregular shapes and skeleton legs. Pay attention to the angles of the rider and horse, the way the rider sits forward, and the positions of the horse's legs.

Step 1

Lightly draw the curved shape of the horse's body at a slight angle. Sketch the horse's neck, head, and muzzle. Draw an angled baseline underneath the body. Sketch the back legs and then the front legs with all four hooves curling up. For the rider, draw a round head above the neck with a face cross and pointed chin. Sketch the spine, chest, and hips on an angle. Now add the arms and booted leg. Note that the hooves don't touch the baseline.

rider leans fo

hoof curls up

angled baseline

all four hooves above the baseline

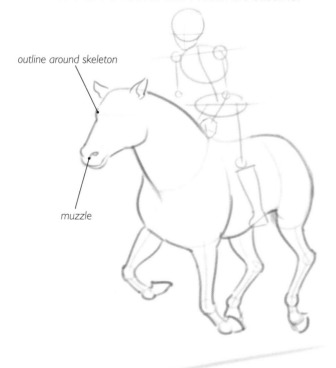

outline around skeleton

muzzle

Step 2

Create the curved outline of the horse's form around the shapes and skeleton legs. Draw pointed ears and define th head and muzzle. Shape the outline of the body, and then the front and back legs.

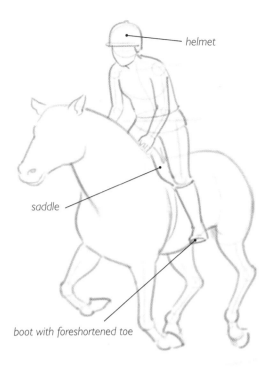

helmet

saddle

boot with foreshortened toe

Step 3

Shape the curved outline of the rider's form around the skeleton. Draw the rider's helmet and the upper body and arms. Then form the legs, boot (with the toe foreshortened), and saddle.

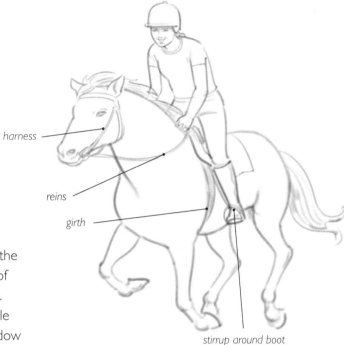

harness

reins

girth

stirrup around boot

Step 4

Draw the rider's facial features over the cross. Sketch the eyes, nose, and mouth. Draw her hair and the details of her clothing. Sketch the horse's eye, harness, and reins. Draw the horse's mane and tail. Now sketch the saddle and girth, and the stirrup around the boot. Add a shadow under the helmet.

Step 5

Study the different levels of shading over the horse and rider. Using light pencil pressure, start at the rider's helmet and shade the light to medium levels of gray tone as you work your way down. Draw the horizon line and cliff face. Once you draw the soft wavy details of the water and the shadows, your horse will be ready to gallop!

INTERESTING FACT → In 1880, Philadelphia artist Thomas Eakins painted *The Fairman Rogers Four-in-Hand*, the first painting based on photographs of horses in motion.

HORSE GROOMING

Grooming a horse or pony daily is a very important part of keeping it healthy and happy. Horses are al groomed to look their best for equestrian events. Grooms use a comb to loosen dirt in the horse's coat, hard-bristled dandy brush to brush the dirt away, and a soft brush to make the coat shine. They might also wipe the horse down with a wet sponge. Finally, they brush the horse's mane and clean its hooves with a pick.

Before You Begin

The horse in this picture is built using a series of irregular and rounded shapes. The girl is drawn using a skeleton. The horse is at a slight angle and the girl is in profile. Pay attention to the angles of her head, shoulders, and hips.

Step 1

For the horse, lightly draw an oval for the head and add a rounded muzzle. Sketch the curved lines of the neck and spine. Draw the chest and belly and add two open legs. For the girl, sketch a round head over the horse's spine and a pointed chin. Draw her spine and legs. Add a round chest and an angled hip oval. Draw her right shoulder under her chin and her left shoulder inside the chest shape. Sketch her arms and open hand shapes.

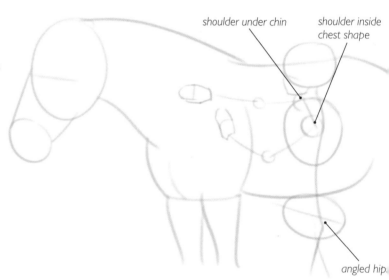

shoulder under chin

shoulder inside chest shape

angled hip

pointed ears

muzzle and mouth

one leg forward

Step 2

For the horse, draw ears pointing upward ar then work your way down the body, drawing the curved outline around the shapes. Pay attention to the muzzle and mouth area. Dr the girl's outline similarly. Note that one of h legs is in front of the other.